world's best
WEDDING CAKES

AMY DOAK

Published by:
Wilkinson Publishing Pty Ltd
ACN 006 042 173
Level 4, 2 Collins Street Melbourne,
Victoria, Australia 3000
Ph: +61 3 9654 5446
www.wilkinsonpublishing.com.au

International distribution by Pineapple Media Limited
www.pineapple-media.com

National Library of Australia Cataloguing-in-Publication data:

Author: Doak, Amy, author.

Title: World's Best Wedding Cakes / Amy Doak

ISBN: 9781925265279 (paperback)

Subjects: Wedding cakes.

Dewey Number: 641.8653

Layout Design: Dustin Schilling

Cover Design: Dustin Schilling

Photos and illustrations by agreement with international agencies,
photographers and illustrators including Getty and iStock.

FRONT COVER IMAGE: NAVY,
SILVER & WHITE WEDDING CAKE
BY FAYE CAHILL
(FAYECAHILL.COM.AU)

BACK COVER IMAGE: ANTIQUE
CROWN AND CORSET WEDDING
CAKE BY SANDRA MONGER
(SANDRAMONGERCAKES.CO.UK)

Contents

5   The perfect cake for the perfect day

6   And then there was cake!

9   The latest and greatest

10   How to...create a marble effect

13   Something new

16   Amy & Joe's Wedding

22   Sweet tips...tools of the trade

24   Love the love birds

25   How to...make a birdcage cake

29   Birds of a feather

31   Ann-marie & Adrian's Wedding

36   Sweet tips...working with buttercream

37   Let it shine

38   How to...create a sparkle cake

41   Shining with happiness

45   Jill & Justin's Wedding

50   Sweet tips...working with fondant

51   For the love of vintage

52   How to...make a simple chocolate ganache

55   Loving the classics

60   Tracey & Wayne's Wedding

65   Sweet tips...serving sizes

67   Love is like a flower

68   How to...create a port wine magnolia shimmer cake

73   A floral arrangement

77   Andrea & Kade's Wedding

83   How to...make an open peony

85   Get a little creative

86   How to...create a watercolour painted effect

88   Express your love

93   Lucy & Tim's Wedding

99   Sweet tips...the ideal flavour

101   Au naturel

102   How to...build a naked cake

104   Keeping it real

108   Stephanie & Daniel's Wedding

113   Wedding cakes of yesteryear

118   When a cake isn't a cake

122   Sweet tips...solving problems

123   Pulling it all together

124   Websites & resources

125   Meet our experts

TOP: STUDIOCAKE.COM.AU

ABOVE: FAYECAHILL.COM.AU

BELOW: JUNIPERCAKERY.CO.UK

ALEXANDRIA FROM THE
CAKE OPERA CO IN ONTARIO
CAPTURES A LITTLE PIECE
OF 18TH CENTURY FRENCH
DECADENCE IN EVERY CAKE
(CAKEOPERACO.COM)

WEDDING CAKES

THE PERFECT CAKE
for the perfect day

There are two kinds of iconic images taken at almost every wedding I can think of: one is of the couple, newly married, walking out of the church or back down the aisle together, much to the delight of their loved ones. The other is of the newlyweds cutting their cake. The cake is often the final moment of a beautiful day – you've said your vows, the dress is divine and all the people who are special in your life are there. Speeches and thank you's are said and then…the cake is cut! It signifies the beginning of the next chapter of your lives together (and, more often than not, time to party!)

I was married in a barn (well, the wedding was outdoors, but the reception was in a barn) just outside a little country town almost eight years ago. My wedding cake, like the rest of my wedding, was themed accordingly. A soft colour palette with the boys and my wedding dress in a light latte colour, girls in pastels and lots of hydrangeas and roses filling vintage tea cups on the centre of each table. The cake needed to be just as simple… but also just as special. So, a two-tiered simple square shape (chocolate Cointreau on the top layer, white chocolate mud on the bottom…yum!)

was decorated with buttercream and lace detail matching my dress and a single rose on top. Perfect. It reflected the casualness of the day whilst still offering a little formality and tradition.

Every wedding cake tells a story and every bride wants that perfect cake to help top off their perfect day…the icing on the wedding cake if you will! I am honoured to be able to share some of the world's best wedding cakes with you. Talented designers from around the globe are creating some incredible cakes that taste as good as they look. The most beautiful thing about all of these cakes though is the fact that they tell a story about the people that they were created for. That is what makes them so special.

So read on and get inspired, learn the tricks of the trade from our experts and see just what is on offer when it comes to wedding cakes - both today and in days gone by. May this help you find and select the perfect wedding cake for your very special day.

- Amy

WEDDING CAKES

And then there was cake!

EVER WONDERED WHY WE HAVE A CAKE AT WEDDINGS? BLAME THE ROYALS.

ABOVE: ENGLISH POLITICIAN, WILLIAM WEDGEWOOD BENN, AND HIS BRIDE, MARGARET HOLMES, CUTTING THEIR WEDDING CAKE, 1920

The modern day wedding and many of its associated trends often hail back to the mid-1800s and Queen Victoria. Whilst she was not the first person to wear a white wedding dress or have a fancy cake she was the first to put it all together and create a BIG wedding. Previously, weddings had been a fairly low-key affair (even amongst royals). They were special days and celebrations but they were definitely more about the formality of the actual ceremony as opposed to the fanciness that we are familiar with today. To be fair though, Queen Victoria's wedding was kind of a big deal – she was the

WEDDING CAKES

ABOVE: MR SCHUR, CHIEF CONFECTIONER AT MCVITIE & PRICE, PUTTING THE FINAL TOUCHES ON THE WEDDING CAKE OF PRINCESS ELIZABETH AND PRINCE PHILIP, 1947

BELOW: ELVIS PRESLEY BEING FED A MOUTHFUL OF WEDDING CAKE BY HIS BRIDE, PRISCILLA AT THE ALADDIN HOTEL, LAS VEGAS, 1967

first reigning queen to marry since Queen Mary in 1554.

Queen Victoria's wedding cake was described by the 1840 Annual Register as "weighing nearly 300 pounds in weight. It is three yards in circumference and about 14 inches in depth. It is covered in sugar of the purest white; on the top is seen the figure of Britannia in the act of blessing the illustrious bride and bridegroom, who are dressed in the costume of ancient Rome. These figures are not quite a foot in height; at the feet of his serene highness is the effigy of a dog, said to denote fidelity; and that the feet of the queen is a pair of turtle doves, denoting the felicities of the marriage state. A cupid is writing in a volume expanded on his knees the date of the day of the marriage, and various other cupids are sporting

and enjoying themselves as such interesting little individuals generally do. These little figures are well modelled. On the top of the cake are numerous bouquets of white flowers tied with true lovers' knots of white satin riband, intended for presents to the guests at the nuptial breakfast. This elegant emblem of the felicities of marriage will be placed on the breakfast table of the queen at Buckingham palace at the breakfast which is to succeed the ceremonies in the chapel royal."

The concept of a wedding cake is traced back to medieval times – made of wheat the 'cake' was actually thrown at the bride as a symbol of fertility. All of the baked goods (cake, bread, scones, biscuits) were piled high after the ceremony (the higher the better) and the couple attempted to kiss over the mound. If they managed to do so without toppling the pile, they were assured a lifetime of prosperity. It was this tradition that evolved into today's couples 'feeding' each other the first slice of cake.

In the 1600s a French chef visiting Britain was quite appalled by the piles and recommended a more elegant method to stack – using sawn off broom handles to create tiers. This idea didn't really catch on until much later though. In fact the story of the tiered wedding cake as we know it comes from the legend of an 18th century baker's apprentice. He fell in love

WEDDING CAKES

with his boss's daughter and to impress her he created a beautiful, large cake that was inspired by the spire of St Bride's church. However, in a time well before Instagram and Pinterest, we will never know the truth of this tale.

So whilst the British Royal family didn't invent the wedding cake, they certainly made it popular. One of the most ostentatious weddings of the Victorian era was that of Queen Victoria's daughter, Princess Louise, when she married the Marquis of Lorne in 1871. The wedding cake stood five feet tall from base to tip, weighed over 225 pounds and (of course) was finished in fine white royal icing. The first 'public' royal marriage was that of Princess Elizabeth (Queen Elizabeth II) to the Duke of Edinburgh. This was the first televised Royal wedding and the couple had a total of nine cakes at their wedding reception. The official cake stood nine feet tall and weighed a staggering 500 pounds. Their official cake had four tiers and three tiers were sugar replicas of Buckingham Palace, Windsor Castle and Balmoral Castle.

Fruitcake is still a popular and traditional preference for wedding cake in England, Canada, Australia and Southern Africa. Originally, fruit cake was popular as there was no refrigeration and in order to preserve cakes (and all that elaborate sugar art) fruit was saturated in alcohol (whiskey, brandy, sherry or all three) and baked. After the cake was baked, the alcohol mix was brushed over

the surface to both preserve and flavour it. Fruitcakes, like fine wine, mature with age so a long shelf life was recommended.

Traditionally, frosting made from powdered sugar and egg whites (named Royal Icing) was used and as it dries hard, it was helpful in supporting the layers of cake placed on top of one another. Often the columns separating the tiers were broom handles covered in royal icing. Because the icing was so hard, a decorative silver hammer was sometimes placed on the cake table to break the icing and then it was peeled away so the cake could be cut. When glycerin was invented, it was introduced to royal icing and kept it soft – the hammer was replaced by a long serrated knife or a royal sword to make the symbolic first cut.

In the 1960s, an Australian baker created a mixture of sugar, glycerin, liquid glucose, gelatin and a small amount of vegetable fat. The mixture was like dough and could be rolled out like pastry – it took the cake decorating world by storm and these days it's known as sugar paste or rolled fondant. Today, it's the most popular method of decorating special occasion cakes… and as you will see over the next few pages, anything is possible when working with it! Many of the old school frostings and methods are still used today as well as amazingly creative new ideas. As you can see by the most recent royal wedding cake – William and Catherine's cake from 2011 (right) – the sky is really the limit!

TOP: ETHEL SILLBY AND KENNETH HARROD CUTTING THEIR CAKE WITH AN AXE, 1928 **ABOVE & BELOW:** THE WEDDING CAKE OF PRINCE WILLIAM AND CATHERINE MIDDLETON, 2011

The latest and greatest

QUIRKY PATTERNS, MODERN SHAPES AND INTERESTING GEOMETRIC
STYLING ARE WHAT YOU NEED TO CREATE A WEDDING OF THE FUTURE.

ABOVE: TEXTURES & SUGAR MAGNOLIAS INSPIRED BY A BALINESE DESIGN ON A GARDEN WALL BY
MELANIE BYRNE (THEENCHANTINGMERCHANTCO.COM)

How to...create a marble effect

BY **HELEN AT KISS MY CAKES**; PHOTOGRAPHY BY **LEE BIRD**

Helen (**kissmycakes.com.au**) is one clever lady and she loves a challenge. There is no idea too out there for her to tackle and this tutorial – a fabulous marble effect – shows how she enjoys taking on a new concept. Marbling is a relatively new trend in cake design and it's perfect for a modern or classic wedding. The marbling effect is beautiful in this classic black, white and grey combo but you could really use any colour combination and match your special day in the nicest way.

Such a gorgeous tutorial – thanks, Helen!

RIGHT: COMBINING MARBLE WITH A GOLD SHIMMER AND A COMBINATION OF PEACH, BLACK AND WHITE IS A LOVELY MODERN TAKE ON CURRENT WEDDING TRENDS

WEDDING CAKES

1. Create a mixture of black, white and grey fondant.

2. Roll the colours together into a large ball.

3. Start working the the mix using a similar method as you do working dough.

4. Lightly dust your work bench with cornflour, this helps the fondant not to stick to your workbench while you roll it out.

5. After you flatten out the fondant the best you can with your hands, use your rolling pin to start rolling the fondant into a round shape.

6. Be sure to roll the fondant out evenly and from the middle outward. A good way to check is to run the palm of your hand over the entire fondant to feel it is evenly spread and roll it out between 3-4mm thick.

7. To transport fondant to the syruped cake you can either use a rolling pin or your forearms. Be quick and as gentle as possible as the fondant may tear.

8. With your hands, smooth over the fondant to help it stick to the syruped cake then work from the edges downward ensuring it has stuck well.

9. Keep smoothing the fondant with your hands and fingers gently but quickly, until the entire cake is covered. Trim off

1.

2.

3.

4.

5.

6.

7.

8.

WEDDING CAKES

any excess icing around the base of the cake, leaving a few centimetres grace. It helps when you use your smoothing paddles. Find any possible air bubbles and gently prick the surface fondant with a thin, sterilised pin.

10. Using your smoothing paddles start with the sides of the cake and be sure to be at eye level so you can see you're smoothing the fondant out straight. Smooth out the sides to a perfect straight line by using an up and down motion with the paddle upright, then running the paddle (still upright) around the cake. Once the fondant is straight you can move to the top of the cake ensuring the surface is flat and even.

11. Now you have a straight and smooth cake ready to work those gorgeous sharp edges.

12. Place the paddles in a position that manipulates the icing into a sharp corner. Overall be gentle but apply a little pressure on the each paddle with each index finger over the area you are wanting to sharpen. Keep working the icing all the way around but still check the straight lines of your cake at eye level.

13. Use either a sharp knife or pizza wheel to cut off any

excess icing at the base of the cake. You are wanting a clean as possible cut.

14. Use your paddle to smooth the cut edges.

15. Your finished product! Be sure to use a little lemon essence on a paint brush to tidy up any excess cornflower.

9.
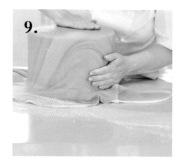

10.

11.

12.

13.
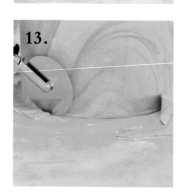

14.

15.

Something new

FOR THAT MODERN BRIDE, THE CAKE MUST SUIT THE STYLE. GREAT ANGLES, SIMPLE COLOURS AND SHAPES THAT TURN TRADITION ON ITS HEAD ARE WHAT YOU NEED.

ABOVE: TWO FABULOUS TAKES ON MODERN DESIGN FROM FAYE CAHILL - A COLOURFUL GEOMETRIC DESIGN WITH THE BLACK, WHITE AND PEACH COLOURS THAT ARE CURRENTLY VERY ON TREND (LEFT) AND A SIMPLE, YET VERY EFFECTIVE DESIGN OF PALE PINK WITH BLACK DOTS (FAYECAHILL.COM.AU)

WEDDING CAKES

ABOVE: NAVY AND WHITE WITH A SILVER LEAF ADDS DETAIL TO THE OTHERWISE SIMPLE, MODERN QUATREFOIL DESIGN (FAYECAHILL.COM.AU)

TOP RIGHT: CLASSIC BLACK AND WHITE WITH A HANDPAINTED GOLD LUSTRE TIER AND BLACK SUGAR FLOWER (KISSMYCAKES.COM.AU)

MIDDLE RIGHT: A QUIRKY BEACH WEDDING DESIGN BY RON BEN-ISRAEL (WEDDINGCAKES.COM)

BOTTOM RIGHT: THE POPULAR QUATRE FOIL PATTERN OVER GOLD LEAF INCLUDING RICH COLOURED SUGAR FLOWERS AND A DECORATIVE EDIBLE TRIM (KISSMYCAKES.COM.AU)

WEDDING CAKES

TOP LEFT: MINT GREEN PERFECTION (FAYECAHILL.COM.AU)

MIDDLE LEFT: CELEBRATING A GRAPHIC COUPLE & MINIMALIST DESIGN (GATEAUX-INC.COM)

BOTTOM LEFT: BAMBOO AND ORCHIDS (YENERSWAY.COM)

BELOW: SIMPLE, AND ELEGANT LUSTRED CHAMPAGNE CAKE WITH DOUBLE BARREL BASE AND DAMASK STENCIL (THECAKECHEF.NET)

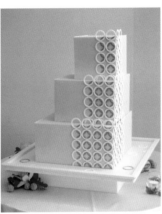

WEDDING CAKES

Amy & Joe's Wedding

WITH A MODERN 'URBAN WESTERN' THEME, THIS CELEBRATION PUT A TWIST OF EVERY TRADITION (CAKES INCLUDED!)

PHOTOGRAPHY BY **MARC ANDREW** (STUDIO306.COM); CAKE BY **ROBIN MARTIN** (GATEAUX-INC.COM)

ABOVE: THE HAPPY COUPLE!

OPPOSITE: THREE OF THE FIVE CREATIVE CAKES FEATURED AT THE WEDDING

"We'd originally only planned to have one cake and in the end we had five," new bride, Amy, explains. "During our first consult with Robin, we realised we had so much design inspiration to pull from that we needed a few more 'canvases' to display our ideas."

The theme all began with the stationary – with a love of horses and Western motifs, she and Joe knew that they wanted to have this as a focus, however the reception venue was modern and so is the couple's design aesthetic.

WEDDING CAKES

"The stationary was designed by my business partner, Amy Steil (mimiweddings.com) and the first piece was the save-the-date that had a modern plaid design and horses. The rest of the details, such as table settings, floral design, day-of stationary and décor, just fell into place from there. With the horses, horseshoes, plaid and wood veneer combined with the modern feel, Robin was able to create five beautiful cakes that perfectly tied everything together."

Amy says the decision to use Robin was easy. "Robin from Gateaux Inc is simply the best. An absolute cake genius. I know there is nothing that she can't do when it comes to designing pieces of confection art. Booking her was one of the easiest and best decisions that we made regarding our wedding. If you have an amazing cake designer, like Robin, push the envelope and challenge them to use their mad design skills. I'd encourage brides to really use their cake as an opportunity to integrate the design details of their entire event...not just their dress. We had a large horse mural in our office that I absolutely adore. Robin had me take a photo of it and then stenciled the exact design on two of our cakes."

"Everyone was in absolute awe of our gorgeous cakes... and because we had so many we were able to give them as gifts to a preselected few. They just loved them!"

"I just loved our wedding. I absolutely adore designing and creating the details for special events, but just this once it was all for my husband and me. Most importantly, being able to witness the one time in my life when all of my family and friends were in one place celebrating together...I will cherish that day forever."

GETTIN' HITCHED

AMY + JOE

7.7.12

MPLS

invite to follow

LEFT: THE SAVE THE DATE CARDS, AND THEN THE INVITES, WERE THE INSPIRATION FOR IT ALL. ONE OF AMY & JOE'S CAKES WAS AN EXACT REPLICA OF THE ARTWORK (SEE OPPOSITE)

WEDDING CAKES

TOP: CACTI AND ROSES SHOWCASE THE THEME – MODERN AND FUN
MEETS SOFT AND PRETTY

ABOVE LEFT: THE MAIN CAKE WAS A SOFT BLUE WITH GOLD AND
TIMBER VENEER FEATURES

ABOVE RIGHT: THIS CAKE WAS REFLECTIVE OF THE SAVE THE DATE
ARTWORK

WEDDING CAKES

OPPOSITE: ROBIN ENSURED ALL THE CAKES KEPT WITH THE COLOUR SCHEME, PATTERNS AND THE MODERN WESTERN VIBE

TOP: METALLIC TOUCHES EXTENDED TO THE MENU, PLATES AND AMY'S FABULOUS BOOTS!

BOTTOM: CUTTING THE FIRST SLICE OF CAKE FOR THE NIGHT

Sweet tips...
tools of the trade

There is a saying that 'a good tradesman never blames his tools' and, given the creativity and skill of many cake decorators, I should think the same could be said about them. However, there are a few handy pieces of equipment that some of our experts swear by.

ABOVE: WEDDING CAKES BY LADUREE DURING NEW YORK MAGAZINE'S NEW YORK WEDDINGS EVENT, 2014

WEDDING CAKES

Agbay Cake Leveller, water brush, and silicon rolling pin.

**Sharon
(sharonwee.com.au)**

There's so many to choose from but the three we absolutely couldn't live without are a set of good quality paintbrushes for fine detailing; a good sturdy scraper for achieving a smooth finish when crumbcoating and a collection of sharp tools such as scalpels, pizza cutters and small knives for fondant work.

**Krystle & Felicity
(junipercakery.co.uk)**

My top three would be my dresdin tool - I use it all the time for making thin and airy sugar flowers, I couldn't do them without it! My pasta roller attachment - using this has saved me so much time when frilling cakes, adding textures and making sugar flowers. I use it every day. Finally, a baker's blade. It's such an important tool when icing cakes to achieve that nice, sharp edge.

**Jenna
(jennaraecakes.com)**

My top three would be mesh stencils - they save me time, and create perfect fine details; my $1.99 cheap rolling pin - nineteen years ago (when I decided to start decorating cakes) I realised that I didn't even own a rolling pin! I ran to the closest grocery store and bought the cheapest pin they had. It is a small wooden pin with worn handles, and I can use nothing else; and a clay extruder - I use this for all small ribbons and edging, and they are always consistent in size and thickness.

**Robin
(gateaux-inc.com)**

" *TAKE NOTE OF THE TOOLS THAT YOUR FAVOURITE CAKE DESIGNERS USE - SOMETIMES IT'S THE LITTLE TIPS THAT HELP THE MOST.* "

I like to use a small range of basic tools as I find this widens my creative options - a basic set of square and circle cutters along with a sharp knife can be used to create a whole range of shapes and forms. I also use a set square and spirit level to achieve straight tops and sides when crumb coating and covering with sugarpaste.

**Sandra
(sandramongercakes.co.uk)**

The particular element of a gorgeous cake that I admire the most is a cake with beautifully smooth and straight fondant, so a set of fondant smoother paddles would be my first choice. I adore creating sugar flowers, so my number two must have is tools for sugar flowers - those that go hand in hand are my foam matt and ball tool to smooth out and soften those petal edges. Lastly my third 'go to' tool would have to be a good quality paintbrush. A paintbrush can be used in a number of ways for painting, dusting dried sugar petals, applying gold and silver leaf and cleaning off cornflower with lemon essence.

**Helen
(kissmycakes.com.au)**

Love the love birds

THIS SWEET AND POPULAR NEW TREND SIGNIFIES FINDING YOUR LIFELONG LOVE AND FLYING AWAY TO A NEW LIFE TOGETHER.

ABOVE: DESIGNED FOR A COUPLE TYING THE KNOT ON A COUNTRYSIDE ESTATE, THIS CAKE FEATURES HANDPAINTED LOVE BIRDS, SUGAR MAGNOLIAS AND OMBRE FRILLS (SWEET-LOVE.COM.AU)

WEDDING CAKES

How to... *make a birdcage cake*

BY **CARLIE OF CJ SWEET TREATS**; PHOTOGRAPHY BY **EXTREME EXPOSURE PHOTOGRAPHY**

Love birds and birdcages have become quite a trend in the wedding circuit of late – and you can see why. Whimsical and romantic with limitless colour options, they are perfect for classic, modern, rustic or floral wedding themes.

The talented Carlie Taylor of CJ Sweet Treats (cjsweettreats.com) has put together this beautiful tutorial to share how you can make your own spring birdcage cake. "Birdcage cakes have been made popular by Tracy James of Cotton & Crumbs," explains Carlie. "They make a pretty cake by themselves or are a perfect top tier of a wedding cake or top cake for a cupcake tower."

WHAT YOU'LL NEED - STAGE A:

- 6" cake of your choice (enough to get four 1" layers)
- 6" half ball cake of your choice
- ganache of your choice
- turntable
- setup board
- 6" cake board (cleaned with vodka before use)
- serrated knife
- spatula
- level
- scraper
- small piece of acetate
- non slip mat

INSTRUCTIONS - STAGE A

1. Trim and torte your cake to get four 1" layers.
2. Trim the excess off your half ball cake and scrape off any 'crunchy' edges.
3. Place non slip mat on your turntable followed by your setup board.
4. Place another piece of non slip mat on your setup board followed by your 6" cake board.
5. Spread ganache on cake board and place one layer of the cake on top. Continue with ganache and cake until you have used up all your layers of cake (besides the dome).

WEDDING CAKES

6. Check to make sure your cake is level then proceed to apply ganache to the outside of the cake, scrape off any excess.

7. Place your half ball cake on top and cover with ganache. Scrape off excess ganache. Continue applying ganache and scraping off the excess until you are satisfied with the finish. You can use a piece of acetate to help get a smooth finish on the dome.

8. Leave to set overnight.

WHAT YOU'LL NEED - STAGE B:

- your ganached cake
- sugar syrup
- pastry brush
- fondant
- cake board
- rolling pin
- cornflour
- smoothers
- pizza cutter or knife
- small piece of acetate

* please note if you are making the birdcage as a top tier of a wedding (or other) cake you do not need to cover a cake board

INSTRUCTIONS - STAGE B

1. Knead your fondant until soft.

2. Brush ganached cake with sugar syrup.

3. Roll out fondant and place over your cake.

4. Gently smooth fondant over cake. Be mindful not to pull the fondant down the cake otherwise your fondant may tear before you get to the bottom.

5. Cut off excess fondant with a pizza cutter or knife.

6. Smooth the sides of your cake using fondant smoothers until you are happy with the finish (remove any air bubbles with a fine pin).

7. Smooth the dome with a piece of acetate.

8. Brush your cake board with sugar syrup.

9. Roll out fondant and place over your cake board.

10. Smooth with fondant smoothers and cut off excess with pizza cutter or knife.

11. Leave overnight to dry.

A1

A2

A3

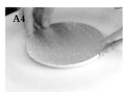
A4

A5

A6

A7

A8

WEDDING CAKES

WHAT YOU'LL NEED - STAGE C:

- your fondant covered cake
- your fondant covered board
- contrast coloured fondant for cage wires
- water
- small brush
- airbrush with vodka (optional)
- 6mm ribbon
- 6mm double sided tape
- pre-made edible lace
- pre-made sugar flowers and fillers
- small amount of royal icing
- shortening
- extruder
- exacto knife
- ruler

* please note if you are making the birdcage as a top tier of a wedding (or other) cake you do not need to attach to a cake board

INSTRUCTIONS - STAGE C

1. Spread some royal icing on the centre of your cake board. Lift your cake off the setup board and place in the centre of your covered cake board.

2. Spray with an airbrush filled with vodka to remove cornflower and to assist edible lace to adhere to cake.

3. Apply edible lace to the bottom of your cake.

4. Measure where you want your edible lace to sit at the top of your cake and mark all the way around. Apply your edible lace to the top of your cake. If the lace doesn't stick, brush a little water on your cake and gently press the lace onto the cake.

5. Place ribbon around the base of the cake and fix with royal icing.

6. Work some shortening into your contract coloured fondant. Roll into a sausage and insert it into your extruder with a fitting to make a thin round strip of fondant.

7. Wrap a small strip around a round cutter and leave to dry, this will be applied to the top of the cake later.

8. Apply water with a small brush where you want your cage wires to be and apply the strips of fondant accordingly cutting off the excess at the bottom of the cake.

 B1
 B2
 B3
 B4
 B5
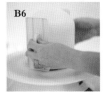 B6
 B7
 B8
 B9
 B10

WEDDING CAKES

9. Measure the gaps between the cage wires and cut enough fondant strips to go around the cake. Apply the strips with water.

10. Roll a small amount of the contrast coloured fondant into a ball and flatten slightly. Attach to the top of the cake with water. Make an indent in the top for the hook ring to sit.

11. Start placing your flowers using royal icing to adhere.

12. Place your hook ring on the top of your cake using royal icing before you arrange any flowers on the top of your birdcage.

13. Continue arranging flowers until you achieve the look you want.

14. Apply double sided tape to your 6mm ribbon and adhere to the edge of your cake board. Voila! You have a birdcage wedding cake.

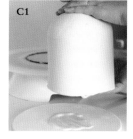

C1

C2

C3

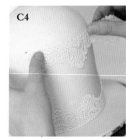

C4

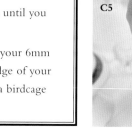

C5

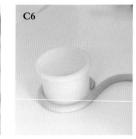

C6

C7

C8

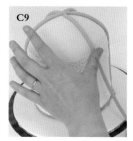

C9

C10

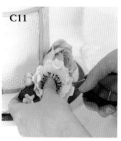

C11

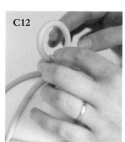

C12

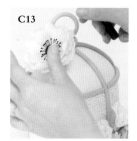

C13

C14

WEDDING CAKES

Birds of a feather

EMBRACE THE ROMANCE OF THIS SWEET TREND THAT CLEVERLY BLENDS MODERN, VINTAGE, FLORAL AND CREATIVITY ALL IN ONE!

ABOVE: A CHOCOLATE MUD BIRDCAGE CAKE & LEMON CUPCAKES (TASTYBAKESSA.COM.AU)
FOLLOWING PAGE TOP LEFT: BIRDCAGE CAKE WITH HANDMADE PEONIES & BLOSSOMS
(FACEBOOK.COM/JENELLESCUSTOMCAKES; IMAGE BY LANE MAULTBY)
FOLLOWING PAGE TOP RIGHT: THE ON-TREND CHALKBOARD LOOK (SWEET-LOVE.COM.AU)
FOLLOWING PAGE BOTTOM LEFT: LACEWORK, BIRDCAGES & LOVEBIRDS ADD SUBTLE DETAIL
(ROSALINDMILLERCAKES.COM)
FOLLOWING PAGE BOTTOM RIGHT: HANDPAINTED HUMMINGBIRD CAKE
(ZOECLARKCAKES.COM)

WEDDING CAKES

WEDDING CAKES

LEFT: A GLORIOUS PEACOCK CAKE - AND YES, THE PEACOCK IS EDIBLE! (BAKERYTREATZ.COM)

BELOW LEFT: RICK ALLEN ART INSPIRED THE RELATIONSHIP AND THE CAKE (GATEAUX-INC.COM)

BELOW RIGHT: BIRDCAGE CAKE WITH ROSES AND IVY (RACHELLES.CO.UK)

BOTTOM RIGHT: A SWEET 60S VIBE FROM THIS LOVEBIRDS CAKE (RACHELLES.CO.UK)

WEDDING CAKES

TOP LEFT: 'JUST US' LOVE BIRDS CAKE (CHOCCYWOCCYDOODAH.COM;
PHOTOGRAPHY BY TINO & PIP)

ABOVE LEFT: LOVE BIRDS UNDER A SWEET FLORAL ARCH
(YENERSWAY.COM)

ABOVE RIGHT: LOVE BIRDS, BIRDCAGES AND BLOSSOMS
(FAYECAHILL.COM.AU)

RIGHT: A BEAUTIFULLY SWEET LOVE BIDS CAKE (SHARONWEE.COM.AU)

Ann-marie & Adrian's Wedding

VINTAGE LOVE BIRDS SET THE TONE FOR THIS ROMANTIC WEDDING IN ITS PRETTY EAST YORKSHIRE LOCALE.

PHOTOGRAPHY BY **MIKE CROCKFORD & GERRY QUINN**;
CAKE BY **JUNIPER CAKERY** (JUNIPER.CAKERY.CO.UK)

ABOVE: CUTTING THE CAKE ON ADRIAN & ANN-MARIE'S MAGICAL DAY

Graphic designer Ann-marie specialises in sweet vintage designs so it was a natural progression to extend this idea to her summer wedding. "I've always loved the Love Birds – or Blue Tits as they're known in the UK – and we decided to include them throughout our day," she explains. "We had Blue Tits on the cake, the table and even a little charm on my bouquet and the embroidery on my shawl."

As well as her design skills, Ann-marie also has a love of papercrafts and she used her talents to create a beautiful rose arch for the chapel. "In the end, I made over 2,800 paper roses for the decorations,"

WEDDING CAKES

she says. "I made roses for the windows in the chapel, the thank you keepsake pockets and the decorations on the candles. The invitations were special to us – it was really our way of announcing to the world that after 16 years together we were going to be married."

Ann-marie designed the wedding invitations herself. "I knew exactly how I wanted them to look and the rest of the wedding really fell into place from there. Our wedding cake was very important to us – we not only wanted the cake to

ABOVE & LEFT: ANN-MARIE MADE HUNDREDS OF PAPER FLOWERS BY HAND TO DECORATE THE CEREMONY AND RECEPTION

LEFT: THEIR WEDDING WAS THEMED WITH GOLD, WHITE, FLOWERS AND GORGEOUS BLUE BIRDS

BOTTOM: A SENTIMENTAL LOVE BIRD PENDANT HELPED INSPIRE THE DAY

WEDDING CAKES

TOP LEFT: THE WEDDING WAS HELD ON A BEAUTIFUL SUMMER DAY IN YORKSHIRE

TOP RIGHT: THE BLUE TITS ON THE CAKE MATCHED THOSE SCATTERED THROUGHOUT THE RECEPTION VENUE

ABOVE: ANN-MARIE CREATED THE INVITATIONS HERSELF, KEEPING IN THE VINTAGE AND BLUE THEME

look different and be spectacular, but we also wanted it to taste amazing. We spoke with a few cake makers but we received the best service from the girls at Juniper Cakery. They offered us tastings to try and every step of the way they kept us informed. In the end we selected a marble sponge – vanilla, chocolate and strawberry – and the cake was the lightest and the most delicious we'd ever tasted."

The two Blue Tits on the cake were matched to the others set throughout the reception room and the roses and hydrangeas complimented Ann-marie's bouquet and all of her beautiful papery work. "Everything was above and beyond what we hoped for. The sketches that Juniper Cakery provided us with were amazing and the cake was perfect in every possible way. All of our guests thought our cake was the most incredible cake

they had not only seen, but also eaten! We were thrilled by the reaction of everyone."

"I would definitely encourage others planning a wedding to ensure they taste the cake – even if they are cupcakes – so you know what the finished product will be like. It's also important to see examples of previous work, or read feedback about the company."

"We wanted a small, intimate wedding ceremony and reception for close friends and family, and then a great celebration in the evening with lots more people and a large party. Our day was the best day ever…I know everyone says that, but for us it really was. We put so much effort into everything – the decoration, the planning, the whole event – and it turned out better than we could have possibly imagined."

WEDDING CAKES

Sweet tips...
working with buttercream

BUTTER CREAM (OR BUTTER ICING, MOCK CREAM OR BUTTER FROSTING) IN ITS SIMPLEST FORM IS MADE BY CREAMING BUTTER AND POWDERED SUGAR. WITH ITS DELICIOUS FLAVOUR AND SOFT, RUSTIC FEEL IT IS OFTEN A FAVOURITE AMONGST BRIDES AND GROOMS. HOWEVER, IT CAN BE VERY TRICKY TO WORK WITH!

What works best for me (after a lot of trial and error!) is to first stack your cake, let it chill, then trim the 'crust' off with a serrated knife. Then, put a good crumb coat on, and refrigerate for half an hour. Finally, put another coat on and smooth it with a baker's blade over and over again until it is smooth. This takes quite some time and repetition to get the smooth sides and sharp corners but the effect is worth it!

Jenna
(jennaraecakes.com)

I use my paddle attachment on my mixer for about 5 minutes and that pushes out excess air bubbles and creates a smoother texture.

Helen
(kissmycakes.com.au)

Make sure you use a good quality buttercream recipe (such as swiss meringue instead of the simpler recipes with shortening). The key is to chill the cake with the buttercream on it to make it easier to smooth.

Sharon
(sharonwee.com.au)

I use softened salted butter (I think salted butter gives the best flavor), vanilla bean extract and I always sieve my icing sugar. I use a hand mixer or my trusty Kitchenaid to beat the buttercream until beautifully pale and fluffy. I also add a little splash of milk to make the buttercream nice and smooth.

Sandra
(sandramongercakes. co.uk)

When we were beginners we found out very early on how important it is to find a butter that will work for you. There are lots of brands out there to choose from so our tip would be to experiment because you will get different results. Once you find the butter that gives you the best results, stick with it.

Krystle & Felicity
(junipercakery.co.uk)

BELOW: A CAKE FROM A MASS WEDDING AT UNIVERSAL STUDIOS, 2001

Let it shine

WHAT BETTER WAY TO CELEBRATE A SPECIAL OCCASION THAN WITH A WHOLE LOT OF SPARKLE AND SHIMMER!

ABOVE: THE BRIEF FOR THIS CAKE WAS 'INDUSTRIALIST GLAM' WITH A SILVER AND GREEN COLOUR SCHEME – THE SHINE IS SOFTENED WITH WAFER PAPER LAYERING (SWEETESTJUBILEE.COM.AU)

How to...
create a sparkle cake

BY **JENNA AT JENNA RAE CAKES**; PHOTOGRAPHY BY **BRITTANT MAHOOD PHOTOGRAPHY**

I am not sure that anyone does sparkle quite like Jenna (jennaraecakes.com). Her beautiful combinations are fresh, striking and modern, whilst still being soft and very, very pretty. A single tier may be all that is required with this lovely technique although as you can see from some of Jenna's other cakes (shown throughout this book) it is beautiful when combined with the simplicity of a plain fondant layer as well.

Thank you for sharing, Jenna!

WHAT YOU WILL NEED:

- Fondant covered cake
- Piping gel
- Edible sequin sprinkles
- Gold dust
- Vodka
- Wide paintbrush

**please note: Not all metallic dusts are meant for consumption. If you're creating a fake tier for display purposes only, then you can use any metallic dust (edible or non-edible). If you are making an edible tier to be sliced and served, be sure to use the appropriate products. Standards and regulations vary from country to country so please make sure you take note of this.

WEDDING CAKES

INSTRUCTIONS

1. Cover your cake with fondant. Put your piping gel into a bowl to allow you to mix and dip with your paintbrush.

2. Using a wide paintbrush, cover the entire cake with a generous layer of the piping gel.

3. Scoop a handful of the candy sequins and sprinkle a complete layer onto the piping gel.

4. You will need a gentle but deliberate touch to attach the sequins.

5. Let the piping gel and sequin layer dry completely to ensure they are firmly attached before painting.

6. Mix your gold or silver dust with vodka until it reaches a thick consistency.

7. Using a clean wide paintbrush, paint this mixture over the entire cake until everything is covered.

8. You may need to let it dry and then touch it up.

9. Once complete, let your cake dry overnight. If stacking the cake, this is a very important step as it will avoid the metallic colour transferring to the rest of the cake.

2.

3.

4.

1.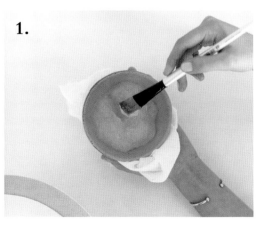

5.

WEDDING CAKES

WEDDING CAKES

Shining with happiness

A LITTLE GLIMMER AND A LITTLE SPARKLE IS THE PERFECT WAY TO ADD THAT SPECIAL TOUCH TO YOUR SPECIAL DAY.

ABOVE: TWO DELIGHTFULLY SHINY OPTIONS FROM FAYE CAHILL - THE LEFT WITH A FULL GOLD LEAF FINISH AND, ON THE RIGHT, A MODERN NAVY AND WHITE OFFERING (FAYECAHILL.COM.AU)

NAVY, WHITE AND GOLD IS
A GORGEOUS COMBINATION
(SHARONWEE.COM.AU)

WEDDING CAKES

LEFT: A TOUCH OF FLORAL & SHINE (KISSMYCAKES.COM.AU; STUDIOCAKE.COM.AU)

MIDDLE LEFT: ART DECO STYLE (SHARONWEE.COM.AU)

MIDDLE: CHANDELIER CAKE (SWEETCREATIONS-CAKES.COM.AU; EMMA NAYLOR IMAGES)

BOTTOM LEFT: ANTHONY CALLEA & TIM CAMPBELL'S UNIQUE WEDDING CAKE (KISSMYCAKES. COM.AU)

BOTTOM RIGHT: SILVER SPARKLE OFFERS A SOFTER FEEL & A DARKER FLORAL ADDS DRAMA (JENNARAECAKES.COM)

WEDDING CAKES

ABOVE: GOLD AND PINK ROYALE CAKE WITH HANDPAINTED MONOGRAM (FACEBOOK.COM/CUPPYANDCAKE)

TOP RIGHT: HANDMADE ROSE RUFFLES WITH GOLD LEAF AND HAND MADE RANNUCULUS (MADABOUTCAKES.COM.AU)

ABOVE RIGHT: A BEAUTIFUL GOLD SPARKLE AND RUFFLE CAKE (JENNARAECAKES.COM)

RIGHT: THE RUFFLES ON THIS CAKE WERE INSPIRED BY THE BRIDE'S DRESS AND THE TOUCH OF SILVER LEAF MAKES IT POP (SUGARBEECAKES.COM.AU)

WEDDING CAKES

Jill & Justin's Wedding

THIS ELEGANT AND ROMANTIC DAY WAS TOPPED OFF BY THE PERFECT AMOUNT OF SPARKLE!

PHOTOGRAPHY BY **LUCKYGIRL PHOTOGRAPHY** (LUCKYGIRL.CA);
CAKE BY **JENNA ILLCHUK** (JENNARAECAKES.COM)

ABOVE: JILL & JUSTIN'S DOG, SEAMUS, MANAGED AN APPEARANCE ON THEIR SPECIAL DAY

When it came to planning her wedding, bride-to-be Jill knew that there were two elements that were going to be important to her: the cake and the flowers. "The very first thing I did was hire a wedding planner!" explains Jill. "Carly of Loulou Weddings was the person who made our day the day of our dreams! She really took our vision and brought it to life."

"I had a clear vision of what I wanted in terms of colour and décor – soft blush pinks, ivory, gold and a touch of sparkle. We also knew that we wanted the Provencher Room at the gorgeous Fort Garry

WEDDING CAKES

ABOVE LEFT: THE ROMANTIC GOWNS SET THE COLOUR PALETTE OF WHITE AND SOFT PINK

ABOVE & BELOW: JILL'S VISION CAME TO LIFE IN THE BEAUTIFUL RECEPTION VENUE

OPPOSITE: THE STUNNING CAKE TOLD THE STORY OF THE DAY

Hotel (in Winnipeg, Manitoba, Canada) to look romantic and elegant. We wanted to work with the intricate gold and pale colours in the room, and we also wanted to add our own personal touches."

Some of those clever little additions included the use of wine corks – to embrace Jill and Justin's love of wine. Place card holders were custom stamped corks and guests signed corks instead of a guest book.

Jill loves to bake and she ranked the cake amongst one of the most important things at her wedding. "I had seen Jenna Rae Cakes on various social media platforms and then at a local wedding show. I knew her cakes were beautiful and her decorating style aligned beautifully with our vision for the wedding. After doing some research and meeting with other bakers, I knew there was no one else who could do what Jenna could!"

"We met with Jenna to taste cakes and come up with a design and the cakes were delicious. Justin and I knew right away that we wanted the almond cake with a vanilla buttercream. As yummy as the chocolate and red velvet were, I couldn't get past the idea of cutting into a gorgeous light pink and white cake and then seeing a harsh, dark colour. In terms of the design, we told Jenna what we had planned for the rest of the wedding and then left the rest to her! I knew she did amazing things and she did not disappoint. Not long after

WEDDING CAKES

our meeting she sent us sketches of her ideas and we were thrilled. Jenna made a cake that was truly a piece of art. It was more than we ever could have hoped for!"

"On the day of our wedding we received rave reviews about the cake – and not just about how gorgeous it was. Everyone said it was delicious and one guest even indulged in five pieces! Because Jenna is active on social media, it was lovely to hear of people who didn't even attend the wedding say how beautiful it was."

"Giving Jenna creative freedom as an artist worked out phenomenally for us. I knew

that I had never seen a cake of hers that I didn't like. She knew the colours and the flowers we were using so we just thought, 'let her do her thing.' We knew she would make something gorgeous anyway, but if she was able to have fun and be creative then the end result was sure to be incredible…and it was!"

"Our wedding day was everything we hoped for and more. Our vision came to life in the most beautiful way and it was wonderful to spend the day with friends and family. One of my favourite parts of the day was stopping past our house after the

OPPOSITE TOP: THE FIRST BITE
OPPOSITE BOTTOM: FUN SIGNS ON THE BRIDAL TABLE

BELOW: THE TOUCHES OF SPARKLE THROUGHOUT BROUGHT THE PERSONAL TOUCHES TO LIFE

WEDDING CAKES

ceremony to take photos with our dog, Seamus. Justin says his favourite part of the day was walking into the reception room and seeing it set up for the first time. The room looked beautiful and it made me so happy to see it all come together. My dad had actually given me a bit of a hard time about renting gold Chiavari chairs – 'the hotel already has chairs!' – and when he came up to me during dinner and whispered 'the chairs really make the room' it was another lovely moment. We ended our perfect day having so much fun dancing with friends…it was wonderful."

WEDDING CAKES

Sweet tips...working with fondant

IN ORDER TO GET THAT FABULOUS SMOOTH, PROFESSIONAL FINISH
YOU NEED TO MASTER WORKING WITH FONDANT!

ABOVE: A DECORATIVE FONDANT ROSE IS CREATED FOR PRINCE WILLIAM & CATHERINE MIDDLETON'S WEDDING CAKE

Buy good fondant! The cheap stuff is hard to work with and even harder to eat.

Robin (gateaux-inc.com)

It's important to work quickly and confidently. Mistakes come from hesitation. Working slowly makes fondant dry out and draping it slowly makes it tear.

Sharon (sharonwee.com.au)

Fondant must be really well kneaded and warmed up before use. I cut the fondant into small chunks to make it more manageable then knead until smooth and pliable. A large rolling pin and sugar shaker are essential and I keep rotating the fondant whilst rolling to make sure it hasn't stuck to the work top. I always pick up the fondant on my rolling pin so as not to mark it. Two cake smoothers are useful; you can use one in each hand to smooth the fondant down.

Sandra (sandramongercakes.co.uk)

Use a good quality fondant! I use Satin Ice and it is my favorite and easiest to work with. I've used others and no matter how hard I tried I would always get tears or wrinkles. Make sure the cake you are covering is cold and smooth, and roll out your fondant as thin as you can work with.

Jenna (jennaraecakes.com)

Experiment! There are lots of good, and bad, brands of fondant out there.

Some are more prone to cracking and drying out than others are, some are too sticky and taste can vary widely. Make a pros and cons list and put them to the test; you'll soon know what works and what doesn't.

Krystle & Felicity (junipercakery.co.uk)

I remember when I was a beginner air bubbles gave me a bit of grief and the simple remedy was the humble pin! Try not to pierce the chocolate and cake, just the fondant and use your paddles to smooth over. Also choose the thinnest pin you can find or an acupuncture pin.

Helen (kissmycakes.com.au)

For the love of vintage

OLD SCHOOL STYLE CAKES MAKE FOR A CLASSIC WEDDING
THAT WILL ALWAYS BE TIMELESS.

WEDDING CAKES

How to...make a simple chocolate ganache

BY HELEN AT KISS MY CAKES

Ganache is from the French word for 'jowl' and is a glaze, icing, sauce or filling for pastries made from chocolate and cream. Its origins are debatable (some say it's thanks to the French, others say thanks to the Swiss) but it dates back to the 1850s. The beautiful, shiny, tasty chocolate-cream combo could pass for frosting, mousse, glaze or a truffle and it's been a popular choice for wedding cakes for many years. Helen (**kissmycakes.com.au**) has put together a lovely, simple tutorial to guide you through the perfect ganache finish.

1.

INSTRUCTIONS

1. Pour 600ml of cream that has been brought to the boil into 1.3 kg (3 pounds) of good quality dark chocolate.

2. Using a spatula or whisk (I use a spatula to minimise air bubbles), stir through hot cream until the chocolate has melted.

3. Your chocolate ganache should be smooth in texture. If your ganache is still a little lumpy simply pop your bowl over boiling water. Be careful and ensure the bowl is not sitting in the water. Use your whisk to help get those last few lumps of chocolate to dissolve.

4. After the ganache has set, scrape a little ganache on the base of your cake board with a palette knife to help secure the cake.

2.

WEDDING CAKES

5. Trim the edges of the cake down to allow you to ganache the sides of the cake with your scraper or large palette knife.

6. Note the space I have left for the ganache on the outer edge of cake. Fill your cake with your choice of filling. If using buttercream be careful not to fill right to the edges as the buttercream often oozes out and creates lumps.

7. Using either a palette knife or clear scraper collect a manageable amount of ganache and apply to the side of the cake using the cake board as a guide. Continue all the way around the cake but not the top of the cake just yet, your aim is to perfect the sides first.

8. Once the sides are complete, fill the top and keep working from the sides to the top.

9. Keep building the sides and top until you have built your perfect shape. You may scrape some ganache away and add a little more in other places needed.

10. Once you have achieved your desired shape, use a palette knife dipped in hot water and wiped clean to help polish those edges.

11. Allow the cake to set - preferably overnight. Please be mindful of buttercream fillings in warmer weather.

12. Using a quality pastry brush, gently brush sugar syrup over your set cake.

13. Here is the start to a perfectly covered cake! The more accurate your ganache is the easier it will be to achieve those perfect straight lines with the fondant.

3.

4.

5.

6.

WEDDING CAKES

7.

11.

8.

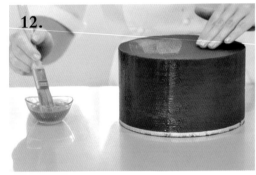

12.

9.

13.

10.

SUGAR SYRUP RECIPE

Using equal parts water and apricot jam bring to the boil. Allow to cool and strain through a sieve. Sugar syrup keeps for up to 1 month in an airtight container in the fridge. STORAGE TIP: Pour the batch into an airtight container. Spoon out what you need into another bowl and brush your cake from that bowl. Pour excess out after you have finished (this helps prevent contamination within your large batch). I use apricot flavoured jam as it's the most mild flavour.

WEDDING CAKES

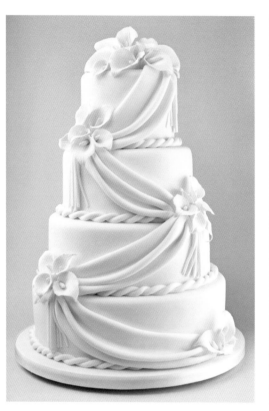 

Loving the classics

SOMETIMES THE PERFECT CAKE IS ONE THAT TAKES ITS STYLE FROM GENERATIONS PAST – A TRADITIONAL IDEA (BUT PERHAPS WITH A MODERN TWIST).

TOP LEFT: BEAUTIFUL DRAPING AND LILLIES PERFECTLY MATCH A BRIDE'S GOWN
(SANDRAMONGERCAKES.CO.UK)

TOP RIGHT: INSPIRED BY THE INTRICATE ALENCON LACE ON THE BRIDE'S GOWN,
THIS CAKE IS TRULY TIMELESS (GATEAUX-INC.COM)

WEDDING CAKES

OPPOSITE: CAKE TIERS STYLED AS VINTAGE HATBOXES MAKE A UNIQUE AND PRETTY WEDDING CAKE (ROSALINDMILLERCAKES.COM)

LEFT: BAROQUE STYLE (FAYECAHILL.COM.AU)

BELOW: PETAL TIER CAKE (FACEBOOK.COM/ MADAMEMACARONGENLAWLEY)

BOTTOM LEFT: RUFFLES & PIPING IN SOFT PASTELS (JENNARAECAKES.COM)

BOTTOM RIGHT: TRADITIONAL WITH MEANING - WORDS OF LOVE ARE PRINTED IN THAT FLOWER! (GATEAUX-INC.COM, STUDIO 306 PHOTOGRAPHY)

WEDDING CAKES

RIGHT: ART DECO INSPIRED CAKE (GATEAUX-INC.COM, LAURA IVANOVA PHOTOGRAPHY)

FAR RIGHT: ELEGANT BLACK AND WHITE (FAYECAHILL.COM.AU)

BELOW: BAROQUE BEAUTY (GATEAUX-INC.COM)

BELOW RIGHT: SQUARE WEDDING CAKE SELECTED BY THE MOTHER OF THE BRIDE (FACEBOOK.COM/ CAKEALICIOUSCAKESBYJESS)

BOTTOM RIGHT: GORGEOUS PIPING (WEDDINGCAKES.COM)

WEDDING CAKES

ABOVE: PETAL TIERS AND
METALLIC PIPING
(FAYECAHILL.COM.AU)

TOP RIGHT: LAURA'S WEDDING
CAKE WAS MADE BY A FRIEND
AND FEATURED HER GRANDMA &
GRANDPA'S CAKE TOPPER FROM
1952 (BROWN PAPER PARCEL
PHOTOGRAPHY)

MIDDLE RIGHT: CLASSIC DETAILS
(FAYECAHILL.COM.AU)

RIGHT: TEXTURED FONDANT
WITH ROSES, PEONIES,
RANUNCULUS & BOUGAINVILLE
SPRIGS (FACEBOOK.COM/
THEARTFULCAKER)

WEDDING CAKES

Tracey & Wayne's Wedding

A VINEYARD WEDDING AND A BRIDE WITH A LOVE OF ANTIQUES AND LACE REQUIRED THE LOVELIEST OF CAKES.

PHOTOGRAPHY BY **MEGAN ALDRIDGE** (MEGANALDRIDGE.COM.AU);
CAKE BY **HELEN CHAPMAN** (KISSMYCAKES.COM.AU)

ABOVE: A VINEYARD
SETTING WAS PERFECT
FOR TRACEY'S VINTAGE
LACE STYLING

"I'd always known what I wanted my wedding dress to look like," admits bride, Tracey. "So, I think that was always in the back of my mind when I was planning for other elements of the day. I love antiques, lace and vineyards so I knew my theme would definitely be vintage with a modern twist. The venue was actually the first major thing that we decided on and that really does set the tone for the whole day."

Tracey says that the choice of their wedding cake was a huge decision. "It's such a major focal point of a wedding. Everyone

WEDDING CAKES

remembers cutting the cake on their special day...not to mention all those photos being taken! It was important to me to have a beautiful cake to look back on in photos. Our cake had beautiful peony handmade sugar flowers and snowberries to match my bouquet. I have actually kept the sugar flowers with the hope to use them on my baby shower cake in the future."

When it came to choosing someone to create that special cake, Tracey says that what she found in Helen exceeded her expectations. "I had seen all of Helen's designs and what really stood out to me was her sheer talent and the passion for her work. She has an impeccable

eye for detail and a real creative flair but most importantly, she listens to what you want. Her cakes are not only beautiful to look at, but they taste great too. We chose chocolate, caramel and strawberry mud cake for our layers."

"My original brief was modern vintage with lace, peachy-pink and black. I wanted something that was elegant and would take your breath away. I left the design work in Helen's capable hands and I couldn't believe what she came back with. She knew I loved lace and that lace was a major feature of my wedding dress. Not only did she match the lacework on my dress to the lacework on the cake design, but she also matched the

ABOVE: FROM THE RING TO THE WINE, ALL THE ELEMENTS OF THE DAY HAD A VINTAGE EDGE

LEFT: CUTTING THE CAKE
BELOW: THOUGHTFUL KEEPSAKES FOR GUESTS PAID HOMAGE TO THE LOCATION

WEDDING CAKES

ABOVE: THE GORGEOUS CAKE FEATURED LACE TO MATCH TRACEY'S GOWN

LEFT: THE SOFT PINK OF THE BRIDESMAID DRESS WAS THE BASIS FOR THE CAKE COLOUR

WEDDING CAKES

ABOVE: THE LACE OF THE INVITES
SET THE SCENE FOR THE DAY
RIGHT: A TIMELESS IMAGE

BELOW: A VINTAGE BIRDCAGE
FOR CARDS
BOTTOM: THE SHIMMER OF THE
CAKE AS THE SUN SETS

luster on the cake to match my bridesmaid's dress exactly. I was so blown away that I cried when I saw it for the first time!"

"I would advise others planning a wedding cake to have a good idea of your colour palette and theme before you see your cake maker. If you have a talented cake maker like Helen, that's all you need! I left the design up to her and she came back to me with a design concept that I absolutely loved."

"I feel so blessed that we had such an amazing wedding day," Tracey says. "My friends and family made our day so special for my husband and me. I was also very fortunate that the weather was perfect and we chose so well with the venue – the staff (at Immerse Winery, Dixon's Creek) were absolutely spot on. My photographer did the most amazing job at capturing our memories and… well…the cake was definitely the highlight!"

WEDDING CAKES

Sweet tips...serving sizes

WONDERING HOW MUCH CAKE YOU NEED? CONSIDER WHETHER
YOU'D PREFER ROUND OR RECTANGULAR...COUNT YOUR GUESTS...
AND THEN DETERMINE SIZE FROM THERE.

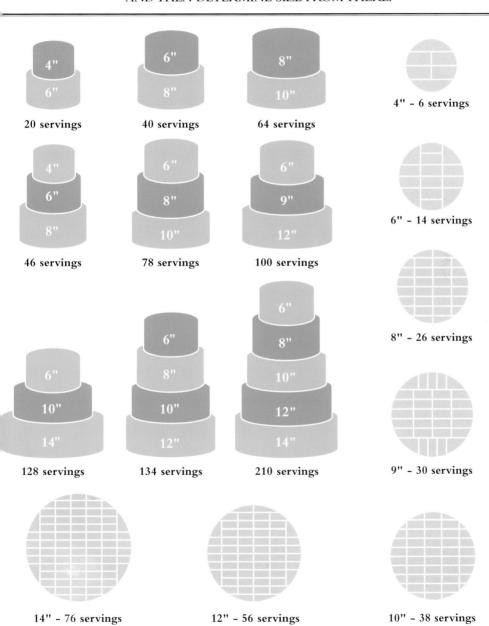

4" / **6"** — 20 servings

6" / **8"** — 40 servings

8" / **10"** — 64 servings

4" – 6 servings

4" / **6"** / **8"** — 46 servings

6" / **8"** / **10"** — 78 servings

6" / **9"** / **12"** — 100 servings

6" – 14 servings

8" – 26 servings

6" / **10"** / **14"** — 128 servings

6" / **8"** / **10"** / **12"** — 134 servings

6" / **8"** / **10"** / **12"** / **14"** — 210 servings

9" – 30 servings

14" – 76 servings

12" – 56 servings

10" – 38 servings

WEDDING CAKES

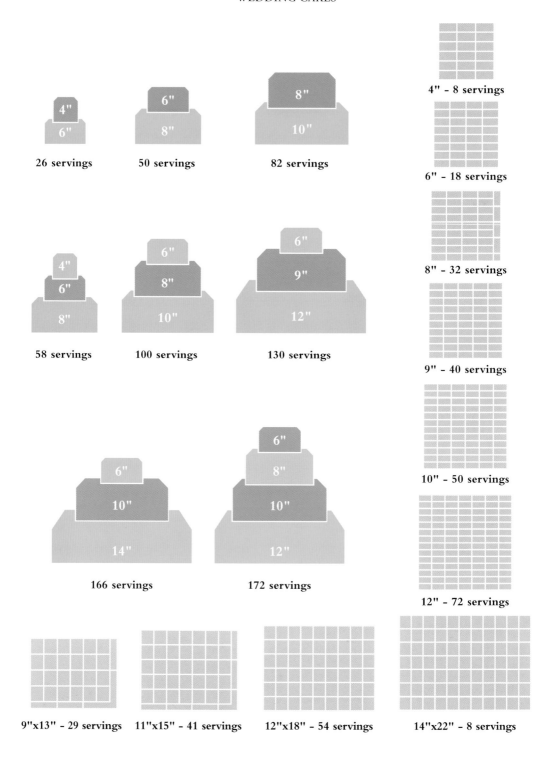

26 servings

50 servings

82 servings

58 servings

100 servings

130 servings

166 servings

172 servings

4" – 8 servings

6" – 18 servings

8" – 32 servings

9" – 40 servings

10" – 50 servings

12" – 72 servings

9"x13" – 29 servings

11"x15" – 41 servings

12"x18" – 54 servings

14"x22" – 8 servings

Love is like a flower

THERE IS NOTHING MORE ROMANTIC THAN FLOWERS AND HAVING A FLORAL
WEDDING CAKE IS A BEAUTIFUL WAY TO FILL YOUR DAY WITH MORE.

ABOVE: EVEN THE MOST SUBTLE TOUCHES OF FLORAL DETAIL CAN ADD THE PERFECT AMOUNT OF
ROMANCE TO YOUR DAY (FAYECAHILL.COM.AU)

WEDDING CAKES

How to...create a port wine magnolia shimmer cake

BY **SHARON WEE AT SHARON WEE CREATIONS**

Magnolias are hugely on trend at the moment and depending on the colour you choose, this beautiful design could be perfect for anything from a beach wedding, through to a lovely country house celebration. The incredibly clever Sharon Wee (**sharonwee.com.au**) has an incredible attention to detail and as you will see from her tutorial here, this amazing cake is no exception.

A modern, fresh take on a floral classic, this cake offers a lovely deep, port wine magnolia bouquet with a rustic, shimmery finish and lace detail – gorgeous! Thank you so much, Sharon!

WHAT YOU'LL NEED:

- Southern Magnolia Cutters
- Magnolia leaf cutter
- Magnolia leaf vainer
- Egg shaped Styrofoam
- 1 x 20g wire (inserted and hot glued into the egg shaped Styrofoam)
- 2 x 20g wire with one end hooked in (for the magnolia stigma)
- 26g wire
- 24g wire
- White Satin Ice Gum Paste
- Green Satin Ice Gum Paste (For this tutorial Americolor electric green, avocado and Satin Ice Brown was used)
- 7" round cake x 6" high
- Satin Ice White Fondant
- Pearl Shimmer
- Wine, light purple, kiwi green, sage green, grape, daffodil petal dust
- Small flat brushes for dusting
- Wide 1.5" soft flat brush (for shimmering)

PORT WINE MAGNOLIA PETAL BREAKDOWN

Bud

6 x 2nd smallest petals (3 will be attached to wires - use 26g wires)

Medium Size

3 x 2nd smallest petal cutter (use 26g wires)

3 x 3rd smallest petal cutter (use 26g wires)

Large Size

3 x 3rd smallest petal cutter (use 26g wires)

6 x largest petal cutter (use 24g wires)

Small Leaves

7 x smallest southern magnolia petal cutter (use 26g wires)

Large Leaf

3 x small or medium magnolia leaf cutter (use 26g wires)

1.

2.

WEDDING CAKES

INSTRUCTIONS

Medium and Large Magnolia

1. For the medium and large magnolia stigma, insert the hooked end of the 20g wire into sugar glue and dab off any excess. Make a long oval shape out of green gum paste and insert one end into the hooked wire. Pinch the bottom and twist with your thumb and forefinger to ensure the paste is secure on the wire. The stigma should be about 1/3 the size of the smallest petal of that flower.

2. Using small scissors, snip the peaks on the stigma.

3. For the medium magnolia petals and the first layer of the large magnolia petals, use the 26g wire. Roll out the gum paste and dip one end of the wire into sugar glue and dab off the excess. Then cut each of the petals and insert the wire between 1/4 to 1/3 of the way up the petal.

Pinch the end of the petal to secure it to the wire.

Use a balling tool to thin and lightly frill the edges.

4. Then use the frilling tool to curl up the tips of the petal. There are two ways of doing this. Either curl down from the top, or curl inwards from the left and right sides. Try to use a mix of both methods so the petals don't all end up looking the same.

5. Use a small balling tool and start from the peak of the petal, pull to additionally curl and make an indent down the middle of the petal.

6. Place the petals on an apple tray to dry. Ensure the sides of the petals remain flush against the tray.

For the six largest petals on the large magnolia, use the 24g wire and prepare in the same way as above and dry on the apple tray.

The Bud

7. For the first three petals of the magnolia bud, cut off the bottom part of the petal by turning the cutter around and trimming off the excess. This will give you an almond shape.

8. Thin the edges of the petal, then use a big balling tool and pull downwards on the petal starting from the tip. This will curl and slightly cup the petal.

Apply sugar glue all over the petal and attach it to the Styrofoam bud. Ensure that the tip reaches the middle of the top of the Styrofoam. Do the same for the other two petals, overlapping each slightly on the Styrofoam.

When finished, the petals should cover the entire Styrofoam piece.

For the other layers, insert the 26g wire into the petal. Thin the edges with a ball tool and then use the frilling tool to pull and mark down the middle of petal.

3.

4.

5.

6.

7.

8.

9.
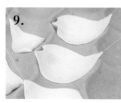

10.

WEDDING CAKES

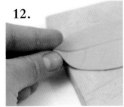

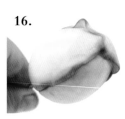

9. Place onto the apple tray to dry and ensure the edges of the petals are flush against the tray.

Leaves

10. Cut out leaves from green gum paste and insert the 26g wire. Pinch the ends to secure. Line up the leaf with the vainer and place the petal pad on top of both and press down firmly to mark the leaf.

11. Use a balling tool to thin the edges.

12. Lightly pinch the tip of the leaf.

13. Dry on the back of the apple tray. Try to dry each leaf slightly differently so they will look more natural.

Colouring the medium and large magnolia petals

14. Prepare the wine, light purple and daffodil petal dust.

Using a mixture of the wine and light purple dust, start dusting the bottom of all the petals. Work on having the stronger wine colour at the bottom and then blending up to the lighter purple colour. Using the flat brush work with long even strokes when dusting. Do the same for the back of the petals. The colour on the back of the petals can stretch a little higher than on the inside.

15. Then using a small amount of the daffodil coloured dust, dust lightly inside the ridge of the petals and around the tips. Try using the pure colour with some of the petals and mix a little wine colour with the yellow with some other petals so it looks a little more natural.

Colouring the magnolia bud

16. Brush some yellow down the middle of each of the petals on the Styrofoam bud. Then use the wine and light purple mix to brush along the edges of each of the petals.

Dust off any excess from the brush then use it to blend the colour from the edges of the petal inwards (towards the middle).

Then mix the kiwi green dust with a tiny amount of wine dust and dust the bottom of the bud.

For the outer petals, mix a small amount of wine dust with the yellow dust and dust a streak of colour down the middle of the petal. Then use the wine dust to dust along the edges of the petal. Finally, dust the bottom of the petal with wine dust and then blend towards the top of the petal.

Colouring the Leaves and stigmas

17. Dust from the middle of the tip and upwards with kiwi green dust, then brush the tip with some sage green dust. Brush the bottom of the stigma with some yellow dust.

18. Mix the Kiwi and Sage dusts and dust the front side of all the leaves. Use the Kiwi and Sage to dust around the edges and in the middle to

WEDDING CAKES

19.

20.

21.

22.

23.

24.

25.

26.

create shading. Leave the back of the leaves plain.

For the smaller leaves, use the yellow dust along some of the edges to create highlights.

Arrange the leaves on some paper and using a glazing spray, spray a few coats over the front of the leaves. Let the leaves dry between each coat.

Assembling

19. Attach the petals to the bud using green floral wire. Try and organise it so that the petals of the second layer sit between the joins of the first layer.

20. Gather the stamens for the medium and large magnolia.

Dust the bottom of the stamens with grape dust and brush the top part with wine dust.

Dip a brush in sugar glue and lightly pat the glue on top of the stamens. Dip the tips into the grape dust for pollen and brush off the excess.

21. Bring the stigma into the middle of the stamens so that the stamens come up about half way. Join both with green floral tape. Use tweezers to open and pull some of the stamens outwards.

22. Attach the magnolia petals following the petal breakdown numbers.

23. Once all the magnolias are assembled. Gather them together and arrange them in your hand and once you are happy with them, bind them together with floral tape.

24. Join the leaves in groups of twos or threes.

25. Arrange the leaves between the magnolias and attach everything together with floral tape.

The Shimmer Cake

26. The shimmer on the cake was created mixing vodka with the petal dusts and brushing random lines with a flat brush across the surface (use the side of the brush to help blend the streaks if needed). Brush the shimmer across the top of the cake as well.

27. Insert and attach the bunch of magnolias. Trim the bottom of the cake with ribbon and lace.

27.

WEDDING CAKES

A floral arrangement

THERE IS NOTHING MORE ROMANTIC THAN FLOWERS AND HAVING A FLORAL WEDDING CAKE IS A BEAUTIFUL WAY TO FILL YOUR DAY WITH MORE.

TOP LEFT: BEAUTIFUL DETAIL AROUND THE BASE OF THIS FLORAL CAKE (FAYECAHILL.COM.AU)

TOP RIGHT: THE FLORAL CASCADE PERFECTLY COMPLIMENTS THE GREY OF THIS CAKE (SANDRAMONGERCAKES.CO.UK)

OPPOSITE: THE BRIDE'S BRIEF WAS 'EVERYTHING FLORAL'! (CAKEDECOR.CO.IN)

WEDDING CAKES

ABOVE: OPEN PEONIES AND GOLD
LEAF (STUDIOCAKE.COM.AU)

ABOVE RIGHT: MAUVE FLORAL
AND LACE IN SEVEN TIERS
(HANDISCAKES.COM)

CENTRE RIGHT: RUCHING
AND SPRING FLOWERS
(SANDRAMONGER.CO.UK)

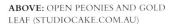

RIGHT: WHITE ON WHITE WITH
MINI CAKES (FACEBOOK.COM/
CUPPYANDCAKE)

FAR RIGHT: BRIGHT &
COLOURFUL BERRIES & FLOWERS
(JUNIPERCAKERY.CO.UK)

PASTEL OMBRE RUFFLES
AND SOFT FLORAL DETAIL
(JENNARAECAKES.COM)

WEDDING CAKES

LEFT: SOFT PEACH COLOURED FLORAL DETAIL (FAYECAHILL.COM.AU)

MIDDLE LEFT: A FLORAL TRIUMPH (CAKEOPERACO.COM)

BOTTOM LEFT: PARROT TULIPS, RANUBCULUS, HYDRANGEA, BLOSSOM & LEAVES (FACEBOOK.COM/THEARTFULCAKER)

BELOW: WHIMSICAL CASCADE OF FLOWERS (JENNARAECAKES.COM)

WEDDING CAKES

Andrea & Kade's Wedding

A GORGEOUS AUTUMN DAY IN A RUSTIC VINEYARD MADE FOR A VINTAGE WEDDING WITH A LITTLE LACE, A LITTLE WOOD AND A LOT OF BEAUTIFUL FLOWERS.

PHOTOGRAPHY BY **TERRI BASTEN PHOTOGRAPHY** (TERRIBASTENPHOTOGRAPHY.COM);
CAKE BY **LINDA COATES**

ABOVE:
CONGRATULATIONS TO
THE NEW BRIDE AND
GROOM!

"When we started planning our wedding, I spent a considerable amount of time reading wedding magazines, scrolling through Instagram and pinning on Pinterest and I was definitely leaning towards a specific theme," explains Andrea. "After deciding on a venue, the theme and the tone for the day was really set. We viewed and booked our venue just five days after becoming engaged. I created a mood board and chose a colour scheme quite early on and things fell in to place quite quickly from there."

Initially, the wedding cake was something that was important to

WEDDING CAKES

Andrea and Kade…but that soon changed! "The wedding seemed to take on a bit of a homemade theme," admits Andrea. "So, I was really delighted when my mum, Linda, mentioned she would be happy to make our cake. I wanted to ensure that I selected something that not only fit the theme and venue, but was also something that mum was comfortable in creating. Naked cakes are quite popular at the moment – and I love them – but there was no way that mum was not going to 'dress' a cake!"

"I am one of four children and mum has been baking cakes since I can remember. Each year we were able to choose a birthday cake from the Women's Weekly Birthday Cake book and she would bake it and decorate it…and she has also made quite a few celebratory cakes for family members over the years. She does a beautiful job so I was more than happy to accept her offer. Having mum make the cake actually came with lots of benefits! It meant I had full creative control and we could really workshop ideas as we planned other parts of the wedding (and I could change my mind at the last minute too!)"

"The venue had old exposed brick walls and timber floorboards, so we wanted to tie in with that. I also wanted the

BELOW: THE OUTDOOR CEREMONY WAS SPRINKLED WITH PETALS

BOTTOM: VINTAGE DETAILS COMBINED WITH FLORAL & RUSTIC TOUCHES

OPPOSITE: A CAKE MADE WITH LOVE

WEDDING CAKES

RIGHT & BELOW: TRADITIONAL FLOWERS AND NATIVES WERE COMBINED AND PLACED IN GLASS VASES AND JARS

BOTTOM: THE BRIDE AND HER BRIDESMAIDS ON THE WAY TO THE CEREMONY

cake to match the colour palette that I had selected for the day. I also love the simplicity and ease of cupcakes...but still wanted the tradition of a cake so that was included in the top layer."

"In the end, the cake was truly a team effort. My uncle sourced the stunning red gum timber from our family farm and my husband crafted this into the three tiered cake stand. We had three flavours – vanilla butter cream, lemon and chocolate –

WEDDING CAKES

so the guests had a selection of flavours to choose from."

"All the guests were thrilled to learn that mum had made the cake and that Kade had made the cake stand. It was the small, handmade touches that really made the day so special…and provided the guests with a wow factor."

"I learnt along the way too! We wanted fresh flowers on the cake, so I needed to provide the florist with as much information as possible – exact dimensions as well as inspirational images. I didn't see the cake until the day and the flowers were going to

ABOVE: FLORAL TOUCHES AT THE END OF EACH PEW

BELOW: STUNNING FROCKS AND FLOWERS

OVER PAGE: BEAUTIFUL DETAILS IN A BEAUTIFUL LOCATION

WEDDING CAKES

depend on what was available at the time, so the more you can plan and discuss, the better the end result is likely to be."

"I absolutely loved everything about our wedding day…but I think the speeches were my favourite. We had given my dad a strict five minute time limit and then he told me he would just 'wing it'…and the words that were spoken were incredible. The speeches from my father-in-law, the best man, maid of honour and my new husband were so beautiful too — I was so glad we had a videographer capture our speeches so that we can enjoy watching them in the years to come."

WEDDING CAKES

How to...make an open peony

BY **FELICITY & KRYSTLE AT JUNIPER CAKERY**

The beautiful peony is a popular choice for a wedding flower – with the scent, colour and softness of a rose but often larger and fuller, it is the ideal flower for many bouquets. In this lovely tutorial from the clever pair that are behind Juniper Cakery (**junipercakery.co.uk**) you will learn how to make your own version of a peony – the perfect cake topper at a floral themed wedding.

WHAT YOU'LL NEED:

- Gum paste
- 24 gauge floral wire
- Floral tape
- Cutting pliers
- Blossom dust (Moss green, apple green and either magenta or terracotta)
- Medium yellow stamens
- A foodsafe fluffy paintbrush
- Edible glue
- Flower forming cups
- Bone tool
- Ball tool
- Blade tool
- Cel Pad
- Foam pad
- Long nose pliers
- Two largest sizes from a peony cutter set

1: Begin by making the pistil and stamen centres to your open peony. To make each pistil take a pea sized ball of gum paste and roll in the palms of your hands a little. This helps smooth over any cracks or creases.

Form your ball of gum paste into a cone or teardrop shape.

With some long nose pliers carefully form the end of a floral wire into a tiny loop or hook.

Dip the loop or hook end of the wire into some edible glue and push halfway into your gum paste cone shape.

2: Use a blade tool to indent lines down three sides of the gum paste pistil.

Repeat steps 1-5 to create three pistils for each open peony you need to create. Leave to set.

Take your set and hardened pistils and bend each slightly outward before taping them together as shown using floral tape.

Now Dust the taped pistils with moss green dust at each base and along the lines that indent each. Colour middles and main body with apple green and then dust the tips with terracotta or magenta.

Take a bundle of yellow stamens and tape into 3 separate bunches for each open peony being made. Take each bundle of stamens and tape around the perimeter of the taped pistils.

WEDDING CAKES

3: For the petals roll out a thin layer of gum paste over a groove in a cel board. When you're able to read text through the gum paste you'll know it's ready!

4: Now cut out 10 petals of the next to largest petal size with the groove of each running down the centre.

5: Dip some floral wire (white works best for petals of a pale colour as green wire will show through) and carefully insert into the groove of the gum paste petal before placing on a peony veining mat to add a realistic texture.

6: Place your petal on a foam pad and thin the edges with a ball tool. To do so keep your ball tool half on the petal and half on the pad as you apply pressure and run the ball around the edges. Add shape by using the bone tool to indent the petals from each scalloped tip to the centre. Remember to add pressure from the tip and then gradually press lighter as you move downwards.

We also listen out for a squeaking sound (which means we've got the right amount of pressure).

7: Leave your petals to sit in flower forming cups or even egg cartons with the scalloped edges curled inwards for shape. When they've set you can dust the centres and bases with blossom dust. To add definition and really bring out that great indented peony shape that you created with the bone tool run a little dust on the tips of the petals.

8: To assemble bend each petal outward slightly with some long nose pliers and tape 5 petals around the pistil and stamens you created earlier. Next attach the next five petals between yet behind the first row of five petals.

9: Repeat steps 4–8 for the outer petals, but using the largest size peony petal cutter.

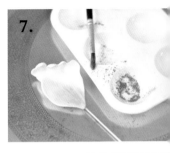

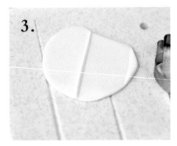

3.

8.

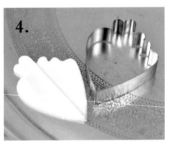

4.

9.

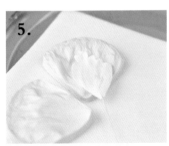

5.

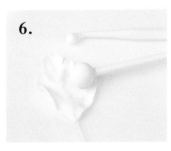

6.

Get a little creative

THIS IS YOUR DAY, SO MAKE IT YOUR OWN! LET YOUR CAKE TELL THE
STORY OF YOUR LOVE AND MAKE USE OF THE ARTISTIC SKILLS OF
YOUR TALENTED CAKE MAKER.

ABOVE: THE FACADE OF EACH SWEET BOUTIQUE HOTEL THAT THE COUPLE PLANNED TO ENJOY DURING
THEIR HONEYMOON IN EUROPE MADE FOR A CLEVER WEDDING CAKE (GATEAUX-INC.COM)

WEDDING CAKES

How to...create a watercolour painted effect

BY **ROBIN AT GATEAUX INC**

Robin is amazingly talented but she has shared the secrets of her skills (and the tools she swears by) with her other business, Evil Cake Genius. To achieve this gorgeous Classic Rose Painting technique, a stencil has been used to get you started.

You can find this stencil (and others) at evilcakegenius.com. Robin has used a Mesh Stencil to stencil the outline of the pattern onto the cake tier in this tutorial. This is a fabulous tutorial for anyone who loves the look of a hand painted cake but either doesn't have the skills or is terrified of the 'hand painting' aspect!

"We created this hand-painted wedding cake for our beautiful bride, Ong, who loves the look of a classic floral pattern," Robin explains. "We covered the bottom two tiers in an ombre of ruffles to lead the eye back up to the handpainted tiers, and accented the entire cake with gum paste floral in matching tones. As a special touch, the bride requested we add her beloved Saint Bernard, Lincoln, to the cake so we hand sculpted him out of chocolate paste."

TO BEGIN:

Follow the basic instructions for Mesh Stenciling on a cake included with the Mesh Stencil, but instead of using royal icing, stencil with a mixture of white petal dust and cooking oil. You should add small amounts of the oil to the petal dust until the mixture is the same thickness as the thinned Royal Icing used in the Mesh Stenciling tutorial (can be found online).

This pattern would be beautiful in any colour, but if you want it to be the same colour scheme shown on our example cake, we used the following petal dusts mixed with cooking oil:

• White

• Ivory (palest, peachy pink areas)

• Watermelon (Darkest pink colour, we mixed this with varying amounts of White Petal Dust to get the lighter shades of pink as well)

• Sage Green (Darkest Green, we mixed this colour with varying amounts of white petal to get the lighter shades of green)

• Gold Powder (mixed with Vodka, and used as highlights on the leaf stems and centres of the lilacs)

1.

2.

WEDDING CAKES

3.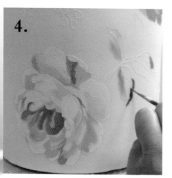

4.

5.

6.

1. Once your pattern is stenciled on the cake, thin down the mixture of White Petal Dust and Cooking oil with a little more oil and use a small flat paintbrush to begin filling in the white portions of the rose pattern.

2. Start painting the areas that will be lighter shades of pink next. The reason we use cooking oil mixed with the petal dust is to keep the paint blendable. So paint right over the white stenciled outlines and blend them into your colour.

3. Fill in with the darker shades of pink, then repeat the process on the leaves, starting with the lightest shade of green.

4. Move onto the darker shades of pink and green.

5. We used Gold Powder mixed with Vodka to paint accents on the open rose centres, leaves and lilac centres. You could do this with the darkest shade of pink or green if you prefer.

6. And voila! Your beautiful floral edible art is complete!

WEDDING CAKES

Express your love

WITH SO MANY ARTISTIC AND AMAZING STYLES THAT CAN BE CREATED, DON'T HOLD BACK WHEN IT COMES TO SELECTING YOUR CAKE. LET IT CELEBRATE YOUR PERSONALITIES AND YOUR SPECIAL DAY.

TOP LEFT: ALL YOU NEED IS LOVE (CHOCCYWOCCYDOODAH.COM; IMAGE BY ANDREW PERRIS)
OPPOSITE TOP LEFT: PASSIONATE RED (WEDDINGCAKES.COM)
OPPOSITE TOP RIGHT: LONDON CAKE (RACHELLES.CO.UK)
OPPOSITE BOTTOM LEFT: TEAPOT CAKE (SANDRAMONGERCAKES.CO.UK)
OPPOSITE BOTTOM RIGHT: MADE FOR RENOWNED PALETTE KNIFE ARTISTS IN PUNE CITY
(CAKEDECOR.CO.IN)

WEDDING CAKES

WEDDING CAKES

ABOVE: HANDPAINTED CAKE (FAYECAHILL.COM.AU)

LEFT: A LITTLE GOTH (YENERSWAY.COM)

BELOW LEFT: WE GO TOGETHER LIKE MILK & COOKIES (SWEETBAKES.NET.AU)

BELOW MIDDLE: SIGNFICANT LANDMARKS CELEBRATED (GATEAUX-INC.COM)

BELOW RIGHT: THE SYMBOL OF A MAN'S LOVE (GATEAUX-INC.COM)

WEDDING CAKES

ABOVE: HANDPAINTED CAKE
WITH SILVER LEAF AND
ANEMONE SUGAR FLOWERS
(MADABOUTCAKES.COM.AU)

ABOVE MIDDLE: OPPOSITES
ATTRACT (FAYECAHILL.COM.AU)

ABOVE RIGHT: THE STORY OF
THEIR LOVE (GATEAUX-INC.COM)

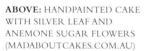

RIGHT: INSPIRED BY THE SEA
(GATEAUX-INC.COM)

BELOW: BUTTERFLY
COMMITMENT CAKE
(EMMAJSCAKES.COM.AU)

WEDDING CAKES

TOP LEFT: MAGICAL CASTLE (YENERSWAY.COM)

TOP RIGHT: A GOLD AND WHITE DRAMATIC SCULPTURE (CAKEOPERACO.COM)

ABOVE: VENETIAN CARNIVALE (CAKEOPERACO.COM)

ABOVE RIGHT: TRADITIONAL FROM THE FRONT...AND A LOVE OF BATMAN FROM BEHIND! (DUBBOCAKEDEZINES.COM.AU)

WEDDING CAKES

Lucy & Tim's Wedding

A MAGNIFICENT OLD HUNTING LODGE SET THE SCENE FOR THIS QUIRKY AND FABULOUSLY CREATIVE WEDDING DAY.

PHOTOGRAPHY BY **OLIVER BURNSIDE PHOTOGRAPHY** (OLIVERBURNSIDE.COM);
CAKE BY **SANDRA MONGER** (SANDRAMONGERCAKES.CO.UK)

ABOVE: THE PERFECT LOCATION FOR A UNIQUE AND SPECIAL DAY

"The venue is what started it all," says Lucy about her wedding to husband, Tim, at the fabulous Maunsel House in Somerset, UK. "It was really the most important part of the whole event for us. We knew we wanted a big country house, and we knew we wanted to be able to make it our own for the day. It was important to us to keep the whole wedding in one place and make a real party weekend out of it. There were lots of cottages on site that we were able to spend the night before in, as well as having the grounds privately on the day of the wedding. Having all our friends spend that time with us was really

A LITTLE SHINE, A LITTLE
COLOUR, A LITTLE RUSTIC
TOUCH AND A LOT OF
CREATIVITY

WEDDING CAKES

LEFT: TAGS TO DIRECT GUESTS TO THEIR SEATS

BELOW: LUCY & TIM MADE USE OF EVERY CORNER OF THIS SPECIAL SPACE

When it came to finding Sandra, it seems that perhaps she found Lucy and Tim! "We looked at local cake makers in the beginning, but we just couldn't find anything that matched the standard we were after. We then looked at other cakes that had featured at Maunsel House and Sandra's name just kept coming up on all of the cakes that we admired. So, we sent her an email and thankfully she was available. When we met her for the first time, she was wonderful. She was so open to our ideas and genuinely excited to try new things. We knew instantly she would help us create what we wanted."

In determining a brief for the cake, Lucy and Tim had one

pecial. I remember the day of our first viewing – we'd driven over three hours to get there – and when we arrived I went straight to the powder room to freshen up…and burst into tears! I knew this was the one. It had so much character and was filled with all sorts of quirky bits and bobs."

"Our cake was very important

to us as well. It was actually one of our biggest worries. I think we spent more time on that than anything else. We used Pinterest and pulled together hundreds of elements that we liked, and then started narrowing them down considering what would work well with the venue, the time of year and also the colours we planned to use on the day."

95

WEDDING CAKES

ABOVE: LUCY'S FLORIST WORKED WITH SANDRA ON THE CAKE

LEFT: THE STUNNING VENUE WAS THE PERFECT SETTING FOR A DRAMATIC AND COLOURFUL DAY

OPPOSITE TOP: THE HAPPY COUPLE

OPPOSITE BOTTOM: CUTTING THE CAKE

WEDDING CAKES

important thing to consider...
"The cake needed to be big! We planned to serve it as dessert to save costs, so we needed it to be big enough to feed our guests during the day, but also ensure there was enough left over for evening guests. We also wanted it to be spectacular – and not to be lost in the background. Sandra was amazing. She sent us endless design ideas and provided inspiration to expand on our ideas. She shared new techniques with us and we were still

discussing new designs less than three weeks before the big day."

In the end, the cake was everything Lucy and Tim hoped for – amazing, beautiful and individual...just like the rest of the wedding! "The flavours were also fantastic. Victoria Sponge, Red Velvet, Chocolate Spiced Fruit Cake and Lemon Drizzle."

"I would definitely advise others planning a wedding to allow for a lot of time when it comes to planning the perfect

WEDDING CAKES

RIGHT: HAND STAMPED PLACE TAGS

BELOW: THE FABULOUS RECEPTION ROOM

BOTTOM: PART OF THE GROUNDS AT MAUNSEL HOUSE

cake. Do a lot of research and don't be afraid to ask questions. Make the most of your cake designer – they are there to help you!"

"All of our suppliers were amazing actually. Our florist, Dinah, worked with Sandra on the cake. She brought as much as she could from the outside, inside. She used the Maunsel Estate to supply the log for the base of the cake. She even wandered around the grounds of the estate collecting feathers to use as the cake topper and she found the shot gun cases that we used for the men's button holes. Our photographer, Oliver, really captured the atmosphere as well as the venue and the guests. Roaring fires, doves roosting, guests laughing, the peacocks, the preparation to the pre wedding drinking that began in the bar…he captured so many moments – even some we missed – and that is really special."

Sweet tips...the ideal flavour

HOW YOUR CAKE TASTES IS JUST AS IMPORTANT AS HOW IT LOOKS! THE FLAVOUR
YOU CHOOSE WILL IMPACT THE DESIGN, AS WELL AS HOW MUCH YOU AND YOUR
GUESTS ENJOY IT. WE ASKED OUR EXPERTS ABOUT THEIR FAVOURITE...

The perfect flavour depends on the couple's preference but my favourites are chocolate mud, red velvet, and lemon and lime. Consistency is important as it needs to be firm enough to hold stacked tiers so denser recipes are better.

**Sharon
(sharonwee.com.au)**

When the bride and groom are choosing their cake flavours, I advise of the most popular flavours of past weddings or 'crowd pleasers' such as chocolate mud. I also add my personal favourites which are caramel mud cake and raspberry mud cake. White chocolate mud cake is also popular as it is more subtle in flavour and not as decadent as the dark chocolate mud option.

**Helen
(kissmycakes.com.au)**

I actually don't like chocolate! So that's automatically out. My favourite cake is our wildberry sponge cake with vanilla bean buttercream. It's light and moist and extremely fresh tasting. It's one of our most popular!

**Jenna
(jennaraecakes.com)**

I am a chocaholic so for me it has to be dark chocolate cake layered with creamy milk chocolate ganache! I love to add flavours to my chocolate cake too – orange, hazelnut and almond are some of my favourites. Cake with a firm, moist texture is best for fondant covered cakes.

**Sandra
(sandramongercakes.co.uk)**

Why choose just one flavour? There are multiple tiers, so I say, multiple flavours. It keeps brides and grooms from having to play it safe with one crowd-pleasing flavour.

Robin (gateaux-inc.com)

We're asked to create lots of different flavour combinations by our clients but fresh cream, fresh fruit and cream cheese fillings are the most difficult to work with. Anything with a naturally soft consistency makes everything from stacking the cake to displaying the cake much harder.

**Krystle & Felicity
(junipercakery.co.uk)**

WEDDING CAKES

Au naturel

ANOTHER POPULAR TREND AT THE MOMENT IS RUSTIC – THAT EASY GOING, RELAXED, MODERN YET VINTAGE COUNTRY STYLE. AND WHEN IT COMES TO RUSTIC STYLE CAKES...ANYTHING GOES!

THIS PAGE: A RUSTIC FINISH (SANDRAMONGERCAKES.CO.UK)
OPPOSITE TOP LEFT: FOUR TIERS OF INDIVIDUAL FLAVOUR (KISSMYCAKES.COM.AU)
OPPOSITE TOP RIGHT: BURLAP DETAIL ON FOUR TIERS (DEESSPECIALTYCAKES.COM)
OPPOSITE BOTTOM LEFT: NAKED CAKE (FAYECAHILL.COM.AU)
OPPOSITE BOTTOM RIGHT: A FRESH AND LIGHT NAKED CAKE (JUNIPERCAKERY.CO.UK)

WEDDING CAKES

How to...
build a naked cake

BY **SANDRA AT SANDRA MONGER CAKES** ; PHOTOGRAPHY BY **ROBIN PAKES**

Sandra (**sandramongetcakes.co.uk**) has perhaps created every variety of cake that you can imagine, but it was one of the latest wedding trends that we were keen for her to share with us – the naked cake! So called because it is 'nude' of the traditional icing that most wedding cakes have, this style has been embraced by brides and grooms looking for a more rustic and relaxed style. Often covered with a sprinkle of icing sugar or loosely spattered with buttercream, you will generally find a naked cake covered in flowers of the season or, such as this delicious offering, with beautifully fresh fruit. Yum!

"This 2015 favourite is easy to make and perfect for an informal summer wedding," Sandra says. "A classic combo of moist vanilla sponge and lashings of scrummy jam and buttercream is sandwiched into deep tiers and dusted with icing sugar before being decorated with delicious soft summer berries."

TIP – Naked cakes are best assembled as close to the event as possible to keep them fresh and to prevent drying. The sponge layers can be baked ahead of time and frozen until required. It is easier to work with semi-frozen or refrigerated layers as it helps keep the crumb intact when trimming and spreading.

YOU WILL NEED:

- 4 layers of 6 inch vanilla sponge cake and 4 layers of 8 inch vanilla sponge cake
- 1 quantity of vanilla buttercream
- 1 quantity of vanilla syrup
- 1 jar of strawberry or seedless raspberry jam
- icing sugar for dusting
- fresh berries of your choice, washed and dried thoroughly on kitchen paper
- 6 and 8 inch round hardboard
- cake dowels
- palette knife
- serrated knife
- 10 inch base drum board or cake stand

WEDDING CAKES

1. Trim and level the cake layers with the serrated knife, gently brushing off any loose crumb. Place the bottom layer of one tier onto the same sized hardboard and drizzle with a little vanilla syrup.

2. Spread the buttercream and jam onto the layer. Position the next same sized layer on top, drizzle with vanilla syrup and spread with jam and buttercream. Position the third layer and drizzle and spread. Flip the top layer over so that the bottom baked surface is uppermost and position it on top of the assembled layers to complete the tier. Once the tier is assembled, extra jam can be piped between the layers to form a soft oozing look. Repeat these steps for each of the next tiers.

3. Dowel the bottom tier with at least 5 cake dowels. If the cake is larger or has more tiers, hollow cake dowels should be used for extra stability. The cake tiers should be stacked onto the cake stand or base drum board at the venue as this style of cake is not suitable for transportation once it is assembled.

4. Dust the cake with icing sugar and decorate with your choice of summer berries.

WEDDING CAKES

Keeping it real

THE RUSTIC TREND EMBRACES IDEAS SUCH AS THE USE OF CHOCOLATE AND
DARK FROSTINGS IN MATT FINISHES, BEAUTIFUL NAKED CAKES COVERED IN
FLOWERS OR BERRIES, OR KEEPING WITH A WOODLAND THEME. GORGEOUS!

ABOVE: BLACK & GOLD RUSTIC CAKE (EMMAJSCAKES.COM.AU; RECORD MAKERS PHOTOGRAPHY)
OPPOSITE TOP LEFT: RUSTIC STYLING (FAYECAHILL.COM.AU)
OPPOSITE TOP RIGHT: CHALKBOARD CAKE WITH SUGAR BLOSSOMS & BERRIES (SUGARBEECAKES.COM.AU)
OPPOSITE BOTTOM LEFT: RUSTIC BUTTERCREAM WITH HANDMADE PEONY, ANEMONE & ROSEBUD
(FACEBOOK.COM/JENELLESCUSTOMCAKES)
OPPOSITE BOTTOM RIGHT: NAKED CAKE (MISSSUGARWHIPS.COM.AU)

WEDDING CAKES

WEDDING CAKES

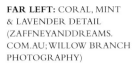

FAR LEFT: CORAL, MINT & LAVENDER DETAIL (ZAFFNEYANDDREAMS. COM.AU; WILLOW BRANCH PHOTOGRAPHY)

LEFT: LARGE CHOCOLATE CAKE AND INDIVIDUAL CAKE BOXES (SWEETESTJUBILEE.COM.AU)

BOTTOM LEFT: ROSE PETAL RUFFLES & DAVID AUSTIN ROSES (WWW.CAKESBYSERENE.COM)

BELOW: TREE TRUNK CAKE (SWEETCREATIONS.COM.AU)

BOTTOM: BUTTERCREAM & FLOWERS (SHARONWEE.COM.AU)

OPPOSITE PAGE: NAKED CAKE (SWEETBAKES.NET.AU)

WEDDING CAKES

Stephanie & Daniel's Wedding

PHOTOGRAPHY BY **NAV A PHOTOGRAPHY** (NAVAPHOTOGRAPHY.COM.AU);
CAKE BY **SHARON WEE CREATIONS** (SHARONWEE.COM.AU)

ABOVE: THE PERFECT IMAGE FROM A MAGICAL WOODLAND WEDDING

A simple rustic woodland theme was ideal for this down to earth couple (and their pet rabbit!).

Most couples start their planning with the perfect dress…or a colour scheme…or perhaps a fabulous venue that needs booking in advance. Stephanie and Daniel, like so much of their wedding, took a unique start to their wedding day adventure. "We actually hired a vintage photo booth," laughs Stephanie. "We had met the owners at a music festival a few years back and we knew we wanted them at our wedding! We secured them almost two years before our

WEDDING CAKES

ABOVE: INSPECTING THE ARTWORK

LEFT: STEPHANIE WITH HER GOOD FRIEND AND CAKE MAKER, SHARON WEE

WEDDING CAKES

for their special creation. "Sharon and I have been close friends for over 15 years. We met in high school in Vietnam and have kept in touch over the years – despite living in several different countries. We finally found ourselves both in the same place and I have watched her grow her business from a hobby into an amazing company. For us, there was never, ever another choice of cake designer."

"Daniel and I have such trust in Sharon's abilities that all we did was choose two of her previous cake designs that we loved and told her to merge the two to create our cake. We told her our theme, and we said we wanted our pets as cake toppers. Everything else, we left up to her. Each tier was a different flavor and everyone could not stop talking about how delicious the cake was – there was nothing left at the end of the night!"

"Knowing that one of our dearest friends was able to contribute to such a central part of our wedding made us so grateful for having her in our lives. In the end, it wasn't so much about the cake but more about what the cake represented to us. Sharon is all about the details and it's those things that often make the biggest impact. She made the miniature replicas of our pets as cake toppers and she matched the exact brindle colouring of our Staffordshire terrier and his lack of left eye, and the oversized ears of our

wedding – even before we had a date or venue. As it turns out, the photobooth was a beautiful addition to our décor and everyone loved taking a photo strip for our guest book."

Following their photobooth acquisition, the couple then booked a beautiful location in the gorgeous Hunter Valley – a beautiful part of Australia. "We wanted a down to earth wedding

that celebrated our personalities and also complemented our wine country locale," explains Stephanie. "We took our woodland inspiration from our pet rabbit, Anarchy, and went from there."

The wedding cake was an important element of the day to Stephanie and Daniel, but Stephanie knew right from the start who would be responsible

WEDDING CAKES

ABOVE: CUTTING THE CAKE

RIGHT: THE FUN VINTAGE PHOTOBOOTH SET THE THEME FOR THE DAY

OPPOSITE TOP LEFT: WOODEN CENTREPIECES AND SIMPLE FLORAL DETAIL ON THE TABLES

OPPOSITE BOTTOM LEFT: STEPHANIE'S BOUQUET

WEDDING CAKES

caramel bunny. Some of our friends even told us that seeing the cake made them tear up because they knew how much we wanted our pets to be part of our day."

"My advice to other brides would be to choose a cake designer you have absolute trust in, and to have a clear idea of your theme. Our entire experience with Sharon was a breeze because we had such faith in her ability and her choices. We knew she would deliver and we just left her alone to work her magic!"

The result of Stephanie and Daniel's faith in all their vendors and their clear direction was a beautiful – and personal – day. "We used local vendors and lots of DIY elements. I made bowties for the boys and I made the bridesmaids' dresses. Daniel and I also made the bunting, chalkboard signs and rabbit centerpieces. The band was my husband and his groomsmen. It was so touching to hear guests say, 'this is definitely a Steph and Dan wedding!'"

ABOVE: DANIEL'S BAND ENTERTAINED GUESTS

BELOW: A KISS SEALS THE DEAL

WEDDING CAKES

Wedding cakes of yesteryear

TAKE A JOURNEY THROUGH TIME WITH OLD SCHOOL TRENDS...AND SEE JUST HOW MUCH THINGS HAVEN'T REALLY CHANGED AT ALL.

30s

TOP: CUTTING THE CAKE WITH AN AXE AT A 1928 WOODCRAFT CEREMONY

ABOVE LEFT: DANCER, AUDREY TOSH, AND HUSBAND GEORGE THOMAS, 1930

ABOVE RIGHT: BIG BAND LEADER, JIM TOSS, AND HIS BRIDE, 1938

WEDDING CAKES

40s

TOP LEFT: ANGELA LANSBURY &
PETER SHAW, 1949
TOP RIGHT: BETTY GRABLE &
HENRY JAMES, 1943
LEFT: ACTORS, JEAN KENT &
YUSEF RAMART, 1946
RIGHT: ACTORS VIRGINIA MAYO
& MICHAEL O'SHEA, 1947

WEDDING CAKES

LEFT: ACTORS PAUL NEWMAN AND JOANNE WOODWARD, 1958
MIDDLE LEFT: SINGER, TONIA BERN AND SPEED RECORD BREAKER, DONALD CAMPBELL, 1958
BOTTOM: PRINCE RANIER III OF MONACO AND GRACE KELLY, 1956

OPPOSITE BOTTOM LEFT: FAN DANCER, SALLY RAND AND RODEO RIDER, THURKEL JAMES, 1942
OPPOSITE BOTTOM RIGHT: HEIRESS, GLORIA VANDERBILT & HER FIRST HUSBAND, PAT DICICCO, 1941

50s

WEDDING CAKES

RIGHT: MIA FARROW & FRANK SINATRA, 1968
FAR RIGHT: SINGER, SUSAN MAUGHAN & NICHOLAS TELLER, 1965
BELOW: ELVIS & PRISCILLA PRESLEY, 1967
BELOW RIGHT: PETER NOONE & MIREILLE STRASSER, 1968
BOTTOM LEFT: ALAN LAKE & DIANA DORS, 1968
BOTTOM MIDDLE: TOMMY STEELE & ANN DONOGHUE, 1960
BOTTOM RIGHT: SINGER, CHARLES AZNAVOUR & MODEL, ULLA THRUSEL, 1967

WEDDING CAKES

TOP: UGANDAN PRESIDENT, IDID AMIN DADA & SARAH KYOLABA, 1975
ABOVE: JULIO IGLESIAS & ISABEL PREYSLER, 1971
RIGHT: CHRISTINA ONASSIS & THIERRY ROUSSEL, 1984

WEDDING CAKES

When a cake isn't a cake

FOR LOTS OF REASONS, SOME BRIDES AND GROOMS SIMPLY DON'T WANT
TO HAVE A CAKE – AND YET THEY STILL WANT THE SYMBOLISM THAT A CAKE
BRINGS. HOW ABOUT THESE FABULOUS ALTERNATIVES?

ABOVE LEFT: JEFF DEWALD & MARGARET NEARY'S WEDDING AT DUNKIN' DONUTS (GETTY IMAGES)
ABOVE RIGHT: A COLOURFUL DOUGHNUT CAKE (KHAKIBEDFORDPHOTO.COM)
OPPOSITE: EIGHT TIERS OF CHEESINESS! (EDPEERS.COM)

WEDDING CAKES

TOP LEFT: FABULOUS MACARON CAKE (JUNIPERCAKERY.CO.UK)

TOP RIGHT: APRIL'S CHEESE CAKE (LAUGH OUT LOUD PHOTOGRAPHY)

ABOVE: PIE POPS (SWEETLAURENCAKES. COM; MICHELE BECKWITH PHOTOGRAPHY)

LEFT: RACHEL & ANDREW'S CROQUEMBOUCHE TOWER

FAR LEFT: CHEESE CAKE (KHAKIBEDFORDPHOTO.COM)

OPPOSITE: OREO GROOM'S CAKE (CARIADPHOTOGRAPHY.COM)

WEDDING CAKES

Sweet tips...solving problems

EVEN THE MOST ESTABLISHED AND TALENTED CAKE MAKER STARTED SOMEWHERE...
AND IT'S INEVITABLE WHEN YOU ARE WORKING WITH LOTS OF OTHER PEOPLE THAT
MISTAKES CAN HAPPEN. SO DON'T PANIC WHEN THINGS GO WRONG...IT'S ALL FIXABLE!

In our early days there were lots of learning curves and looking back there have been one or two designs that would not pass our current standards! We've learned through our experience that being stringent with ourselves is the best way to avoid disasters. Good time management and a critical eye are key.
**Krystle & Felicity
(junipercakery.co.uk)**

One time a venue stored a cake incorrectly and the topper fell apart from the humidity. I needed to go back an hour before the wedding with my fix-it kit and fix and reassemble it while everyone in the venue (both employees and vendors) stood around watching me! And of course they decided it was the best possible time to ask me questions and start learning cake decorating...
**Sharon
(sharonwee.com.au)**

A common challenge amongst cake decorators is how to handle hot weather. It has been a challenge in the past and there have been some experiences that I have certainly learnt from. Having refrigerated air conditioning is always a must when choosing your workspace. Also, be organised for a possible early morning delivery or late night delivery outside of the heat in the middle of the day and give your cake and decorations extra drying time. Humidity beads also work well in small rooms. Have a back up plan in case of extreme heat and have options such as fresh flowers if your sugar flowers melt. Also be sure your cake will not be sitting in direct sun.
**Helen
(kissmycakes.com.au)**

I always carry a cake emergency kit when I deliver my cakes. This includes spare fondant, spare decorations, royal icing, piping bags and ribbon along with a rolling pin, sugar shaker, piping nozzles and cleaning cloths. In the event of an emergency you can set up a sort of field hospital for cakes and do some repairs if required! I live in Bath and deliver throughout Somerset and Wiltshire (which are both quite hilly). I often stack my cakes when I get to the venue to avoid disasters. But if something does drop off en-route, I have the kit ready to quickly stick it back on! I always allow plenty of time to set up, just in case.
**Sandra
(sandramongercakes.co.uk)**

LEFT: THIS IS ACTUALLY THE FIRST CUT OF PRINCE WILLIAM & CATHERINE MIDDLETON'S WEDDING CAKE...BUT EVEN THE EXPERTS HAVE HICCUPS AT TIMES!

WEDDING CAKES

Pulling it all together

YOU'VE REACHED THE END AND YOU'RE COMPLETELY INSPIRED - BUT PERHAPS MORE CONFUSED THAN EVER? LET'S BREAK IT DOWN FOR YOU WITH A WEDDING CAKE DESIGN INSPIRATION CHECKLIST!

It's not always about cakes…have you thought about:

Rustic pies and tarts, cheeses and savouries, ice creams with toppings, lollies and sweets in a colourful buffet, childhood favourites – desserts or sweets, slices, cookies, doughnuts or biscuits?

What's your design preference?

Modern, simple and clean, classic or vintage, bright colours, pretty pastels, fresh florals, glamourous shine, traditional tiers, a cake buffet, cupcakes, smooth finishes, textures or lace, something fun with a story to tell?

What flavours do you and your partner love?

Chocolate, vanilla, lemon, sponge, pound, fruit or carrot cake all make fabulous wedding cakes and ask your cake maker to suggest some variations on these themes for something really unique!

Who are you catering for?

How many guests are you having? Do you need six tiers, or would two be ample? Are half the guests allergic to dairy? Do you want left over cake, and if so do you want it for the BBQ or breakfast the next day…or would you rather freeze it for your first anniversary?

Remember your limitations with icing!

You may love the taste of buttercream but covet a beautiful smooth finish with sugarpaste figurines which would require fondant…be realistic about flavour, colour and finish. What is more important to you – look, flavour or texture? Sometimes you might be able to have all your desires met, but it's good to understand what's possible.

Look at the details:

What do you love about your gown (colour, beading, lace, ruffles)?

What colours are you drawn to in your floral selection (ivory, pastels, bold, fun)?

What mood does your venue create (modern, romantic, traditional, rustic, soft)?

Does your cake or dessert compliment:

Your table linens?

The design of your reception venue?

Your cake topper?

Any decorations or table pieces you are using?

Are you having fun?

It's your wedding! Enjoy it and make sure you eat lots of cake…yum!

123

WEDDING CAKES

Websites & resources

CAKE DECORATORS

The Artful Caker
(facebook.com/
TheArtfulCaker)

Bakery Treatz
(bakerytreatz.com)

The Cake Chef
(cakechef.net)

Cake Décor
(cakedecor.co.in)

Cake Opera
(cakeoperaco.com)

Cakealicious Cakes By Jess
(facebook.com/
cakealiciouscakesbyjess)

Cakes By Serene
(cakesbyserene.com)

Choccywoccydoodah
(choccywoccydoodah.com)

Cuppy And Cake
(facebook.com/cuppyandcake)

Dee's Specialty Cakes
(deesspecialtycakes.com)

The Enchanting Merchant
Company
(theenchantingmerchantco.com)

Emma J's Cakes
(emmajscakes.com.au)

Faye Cahill Cake Design
(fayecahill.com.au)

Gateaux Inc
(gateaux-inc.com)

Handi's Cakes
(handiscakes.com)

Jenelle's Custom Cakes
(facebook.com/
jenellescustomcakes)

Jenna Rae Cakes
(jennaraecake.com)

Juniper Cakery
(junipercakery.co.uk)

Kiss My Cakes
(kissmycakes.com.au)

Mad About Cakes
(madaboutcakes.com.au)

Miss Sugar Whips
(misssugarwhips.com.au)

Rachelle's
(rachelles.co.uk)

Ron Ben-Isreal Cakes
(weddingcakes.com)

Rosalind Miller Cakes
(rosalindmillercakes.com)

Sandra Monger Cakes
(sandramongercakes.co.uk)

LEFT: (THEENCHANTINGMER
CHANTCO.COM)

Sharon Wee Creations
(sharonwee.com.au)

Studio Cake
(studiocake.com.au)

Sugar Bee Cakes
(sugarbeecakes.com.au)

Sweet Bakes
(sweetbakes.net.au)

Sweet Creations
(sweetcreations-cakes.com.au)

Sweet Love
(sweet-love.com.au)

Sweetest Jubilee
(sweetestjubilee.com.au)

Tasty Bakessa
(tastybakessa.com.au)

Yener's Way
(yenersway.com)

Zoe Clark Cakes
(zoeclarkcakes.com)

Zaffney And Dreams
(zaffneyanddreams.com.au)

TUTORIALS & IDEAS

Australian Cake Decorating
Network
(acdn.me)

Cake Central
(cakecentral.com)

Cake Geek
(cakegeek.co.uk)

Evil Cake Genius
(evilcakegenius.com)

Gateaux Inc
(gateaux-inc.com)

The Cake Blog
(thecakeblog.com)

Yener's Way
(yenersway.com)

WEDDING CAKES

Meet our experts

YOU'VE SEEN SOME BEAUTIFUL CAKES, SOME FABULOUS TUTORIALS AND READ
SOME WONDERFUL ADVICE FROM OUR EXPERTS – FROM AUSTRALIA, THE UK
AND THE USA – SO PERHAPS YOU'D LIKE TO KNOW A LITTLE MORE ABOUT THEM!

Meet...Liz Wright

Some of our gorgeous images came from ACDN (Australian Cake Decorating Network) members and with thousands of members worldwide, Liz has created a fabulous resource for cake enthusiasts everywhere. ACDN was established in March 2012 and Liz also publishes online magazine *Cake!* (**cakemagazine.me**) which comes out quarterly.

Becoming a member of ACDN offers wonderful benefits including having your work promoted on their Facebook page (over 130,000 followers); submitting work for publishing in *Cake!* Magazine; receiving discounts at ACDN Preferred Suppliers; discounted cake decorating business insurance through Red Star Insurance Brokers; discounted ticketing to ACDN events; access to the ACDN members only Facebook group; listings in the ACDN Decorator, Supplier or Courses directories on the website and much more. You can learn more at **acdn.me**

"Our ACDN events include Cake Camp," explains Liz. "A weekend away in a luxury resort, including cake decorating classes, meals, networking and evening entertainment and Cake Crawl which is like a shopping tour but for cake decorators! We hire a bus and travel across the city, visiting studios, having demos, high tea, lunch, champagne and shopping." Liz has created a lovely community that welcomes cake decorators from all over the world and from all levels of skill.

Meet...Helen Chapman

Born and raised Melbourne gal. Helen, established her business Kiss My Cakes in 2011.

"I started my cake business from making my son's birthday cakes. From there I was asked to make birthday cakes and then progressed to wedding cakes. I just love creating wedding cakes – I really enjoy the whole proess."

Helen is a mum of two boys and says she loves every stage of creating cakes however designing her cakes and creating sugar flowers are the things she loves doing the most. Working from her studio at home ("It's very convenient!") Helen has created cakes for home grown celebrities such as the recent wedding of Anthony Callea and Tim Campbell.

With the fun of making kids birthday cakes, and the beauty of making wedding cakes, it seems Helen has the perfect mix of creativity and love in her career. "I've always been passionate about cooking and baking as well as good quality produce and ingredients."

See more of Helen's lovely work at **kissmycakes.com.au**

WEDDING CAKES

Meet...Krystle & Felicity

Felicity and Krystle are cake designers and owners
of Juniper Cakery. Based in the UK, Juniper
Cakery is a bespoke bakery specialising in luxury
cakes and confections. Each custom made creation
focuses on utilising their artisanal skills to evoke
glamour, rustic nature and a definite sense of
playfulness that makes their work both elegant and
fun.

Alongside designing and creating cakes, cupcakes,
cookies and macarons they also develop recipes for
the dessert industry, test new and exciting baking
products for large companies, regularly contribute
to a variety of magazines and create exclusive cake
decorating tutorials for Craftsy.com's blog!

Since opening Juniper Cakery in late 2012
their work has featured in both national and
international books, magazines and blogs. They've
created cakes, recipes and tutorials for The Happy
Egg Co., Tala, DK Publishers, Satin Ice, Cake
Decoration Heaven Magazine, Craftsy, Cake
Central and more!

To see more of their beautiful designs, head over
to **junipercakery.co.uk.**